D0426877

That the World May Know

That the World
May Know

BEARING WITNESS TO ATROCITY

JAMES DAWES

HARVARD UNIVERSITY PRESS
Cambridge, Massachusetts
London, England
2007

Library of Congress Cataloging-in-Publication Data
Dawes, James, 1969–
    That the world may know : bearing witness to atrocity /
James Dawes.
        p. cm.
    Includes bibliographical references and index.
    ISBN-13: 978-0-674-02623-0 (hardcover : alk. paper)
    ISBN-10: 0-674-02623-3 (hardcover : alk. paper)
        1. Genocide.   2. Atrocities.   3. Human rights movements.   4. Hu-
man rights workers.   5. Investigative reporting—Moral and ethical aspects.   I. Title
    HV6322.7.D39 2007
    967.57104'31—dc22   2007011216

For Barış, Mikey, and the little one coming

CONTENTS

That the World
May Know

> *Revolted by the images transmitted to us day after day from*
> *conflict zones, at one time or another we all ask ourselves this*
> *simple but crucial question: What can I do about it?*
> — International Committee of the Red Cross,
> Geneva, press release, 2004

This book is about those who decided to do something. It is about their struggle to make sense of the things they've seen, the price they have paid for their commitments, and what difference—if any—they feel they have made.

The events described in this book help to answer two important questions: How do we make comprehensible stories out of incomprehensible atrocities? And what are the ethical risks and obligations of doing so? For many of the humanitarian and human rights workers I interviewed for this book (and the field of the committed includes journalists, teachers, and novelists as well as fieldworkers), storytelling is the very nature of the work. Many of the most

recognizable organizations that intervene in humanitarian
crises do so in large part by using language instead of food,
medicine, or weapons; the most important act of rescue,
for them, is not delivering supplies but asking questions,
evaluating answers, and pleading with those of us who observe from a distance. Indeed, for people in need of rescue
and care, the hope of being able to tell their story is sometimes the only hope. How do you make your case? Get
someone to believe you? Get someone to speak *for* you?[1]

   This book is not about the survivors of atrocity; it is
beyond my capacity to tell such stories with any adequacy.
It is instead about the view of the witnesses—how they
see, from so very close, the atrocities that distantly shadow
our days. Stephen Smith, executive editor of American
RadioWorks, expressed it best when telling me about a
documentary he made for public radio entitled "The Few
Who Stayed: Defying Genocide in Rwanda." The story
focused on Carl Wilkens, who was the director of the Ad-
ventist Development Relief Agency in Rwanda in 1994 and,
according to Smith, perhaps the only American who remained in Rwanda throughout the whole of the genocide.
When everybody else left, he stayed behind to care for the
Tutsis hiding in his compound and to carry on his relief
work. Under fire as he traveled, Wilkens delivered water
and other supplies to a private orphanage run by a Hutu

man named Damas Gisimba. Gisimba was sheltering hundreds of local people—many of them Tutsis—along with scores of orphans. When the militia finally came to kill everyone there, Wilkens confronted them. He approached the leader of the extremist Hutu regime himself, who yielded and stopped the attack. Wilkens was in the middle of the killings; he saw what few in the West would see. But for Smith, listening to the audiotapes Wilkens made for his wife in case he did not survive (his voice mild over the echo of gunfire beyond his walled yard), what Wilkens' position revealed most dramatically was not its immediacy but its distance. It showed, said Smith, "when you're inside a chaotic situation, how without context you are. In his case, it literally is being in a walled compound. And if you're down in there, you can't see what's going on. You can hear what's going on over the wall, you can hear what's happening in your neighborhood, but you're not seeing it. It's very disconnected and very strange, and it's really how a lot of people experience traumatic or chaotic events: from a very limited frame of vision."

That unique position of intimacy and distance, connection and alienation, generates a special psychic friction. You are emotionally involved, but must remain detached enough to operate professionally, effectively, and often neutrally. You are committed to action but, with your narrow view, can never know truly what good or ill consequences will follow for others over time because of what you do. You're there, but you're not really there. "The hardest part," says Karen Elshazly, Senior Advisor to the President of the American Refugee Committee, "is that you can drive away." What right, then, do you have to nominate yourself as the one to tell the story? And what difference can you really make?

Let me start with a brief synopsis of the book. Chapter 1 discusses the stories that have developed out of the Rwandan genocide, and begins with the omnipresent question of authenticity. Who has the right to speak, and how far does that right extend? How are these stories being used, and for whose benefit? What difference do they make? How have we come to make sense of what happened in 1994, and what does this tell us about our collective moral future? The chapter considers legal cases, novels, memoirs, journalism, survivor and worker testimony.

Chapter 2 narrows the scope of analysis by focusing exclusively on ethical conflicts in the storytelling practices of humanitarian organizations, including the International Committee of the Red Cross (ICRC) and the Office of the United Nations High Commissioner for Refugees (UNHCR). How can bearing witness to and documenting the fracture of self in torture both diminish and amplify its damage? How do we create surrogate voices? How must the stories of the survivor be translated, edited, and re-written to fit the officially sanctioned vocabulary of the institution? What, for the organization, counts as legitimate memory in the first place? Topics of special attention in this chapter include the duty to reveal versus the injury of exposure; the various strategies employed for "interrogating" survivors of atrocities; the tension between the subjective knowledge of the witness and the objective knowledge of the expert; the difficulty of communicating trauma and the problem of vicarious traumatization; and the adaptations of organizations to worker burnout and psychic breakdown.

Chapter 3 builds on Chapter 2 by intensifying the focus on humanitarian and human rights work as work. In a letter collected by Médecins Sans Frontières (Doctors Without Borders), one fieldworker describes the experience in these terms: "We are the world's grave-diggers, finding our happiness amidst the growing numbers of massacres and battlefields."[2] What is the nature of this happiness? What are the motivations of the workers, the ethical compromises of the career? What happens to moral passions when they become a job? What are the stories these women and men rely upon to explain and justify their lives to themselves—their decisions to follow such strange paths, and, often, their decisions to abandon them?

The conclusion, Chapter 4, turns away from the field to

representations of the field, to the photography, journalism, and literature of human rights. It is about human
rights activists who have attempted to express their political ideals through art and about artists who have attempted to express their aesthetic ideals through politics.
What do these stories teach us about the nature of sympathy and imagination? About the moral responsibilities of
the storyteller? And what does the development of human
rights fiction as a genre tell us about the future of human
rights as a movement? What can it teach us, right now,
about the work we must do today?

Running beneath this discussion of human rights
fiction—and beneath all of the book's other chapters—
are the crisscrossing lines of inquiry into the relationship
between aesthetics and ethics that generated this project.
How do words move us? How do the stories we tell one
another release our deep emotions—our pity, fear, or wonder? How do mournful aesthetic artifacts acquire the
power to monopolize our regard, to make us gape or
grieve, to make us forget, briefly, that they are only shadow
worlds, that we are not connected to them? I wanted to understand these questions because I wanted to know what
capacity fictional worlds had for creating moral forces
commensurate with their mesmeric aesthetic forces. How,
for instance, might our capacity for sorrow or outrage in
response to an injustice depicted in a novel translate into

our relationship with the social and political world, if at all? Can we better understand how spectators of suffering develop (or fail to develop) empathy for persons geographically distant or perceived as alien if we first examine how they can so feelingly respond to the dreams, desires, and dignity of fictional persons? In *The Defense of Poesy* Sir Philip Sidney describes the tyrant Alexander Pheraeus, "from whose eyes a tragedy well-made and represented drew abundance of tears; who without all pity had murdered infinite numbers, and some of his own blood, so as he that was not ashamed to make matters for tragedies, yet could not resist the sweet violence of a tragedy."[3] What is the line that separates those who are merely moved from those who are moved to act? When does the story become real enough to change you?

This discussion is an attempt to make sense of the violence in the tragedies we hear, and to understand what it is like to be the people who must tell these stories.

■■■■■ The conceptual frame of this book rests on four posts that I would like to describe at the outset in some detail: the ethics of storytelling, the difference storytelling makes, the ethics of human rights and humanitarian work, and the difference this work makes. Chapter 1 approaches these four topics from a broadly public perspective (books, the media, international advocacy); Chapter 2 analyzes them in specific institutional settings (the internal dynamics of humanitarian and human rights organizations); Chapter 3 takes up the personal perspective (how do rights workers themselves experience these issues?); and Chapter 4 focuses on aesthetics (how have artists interested in the representation of human dignity and its violation approached these topics?).

The Ethics of Storytelling

"To write poetry after Auschwitz is barbaric." This quotation from Theodor Adorno has been used for decades to summarize the ethical paradoxes involved in representing atrocity. In giving voice to suffering we can sometimes moderate it, even aestheticize it. As Adorno argues, the artistic depiction of pain "contains, however remotely, the power to elicit enjoyment out of it." Through the stylization of violence, he warns, "an unthinkable fate appear[s] to have had some meaning; it is transfigured, something of its horror is removed. This alone does an injustice to the victims."[4] Indeed, giving voice can also be a matter of *taking* voice. As Antjie Krog writes, using Adorno's declaration to examine her own guilt in representing the suffering of those who testified before the Truth and Reconciliation Commission in South Africa:

"Isn't that a sacrilege—to use someone else's story, a story that has cost him his life?" Yet what are the consequences of respectful silence? There are so many ways to hurt others when trying to speak for them, so many and so unexpected. But is doing nothing worse than risking something? "How else would it get out?" Krog asks. "How else would the story be told?"[5]

This contradiction between our impulse to heed trauma's cry for representation and our instinct to *protect* it from representation—from invasive staring, simplification, dissection—is a split at the heart of human rights advocacy.

What Difference Does Storytelling Make?

One of the most important premises of contemporary human rights work is that effective dissemination of information can change the world. Indeed, the International Committee of the Red Cross and the Geneva Conventions themselves arose in response to a well-told story: Henry Dunant's book *Un souvenir de Solférino* (A Memory of Solferino; 1862), a harrowing account of his experiences attending to the thousands of French and Austrian wounded after the Battle of Solferino in 1859. Individuals can be inspired to donate time and money; governments, particularly those dependent on foreign aid, can be pressured into altering their behavior. As Garentina Kraja, a reporter for Kosovo's Albanian-language newspaper *Koha Ditore,* expressed it: "During the war, working in a paper and reporting about the war was the only thing that seemed to have any meaning. We were reporting about what was happening, and those reports did make a change, I think. After all, I think that the reports of the journalists about the atrocities helped to convince the international community to intervene in this conflict."[6]

Much of the work on storytelling and human rights, however, has focused on the opposite: the *impotence* of representation. Journalists and activists around the world, working from their own experiences of frustration in Rwanda, the Balkans, and elsewhere, have catalogued the many ways stories designed to shake us out of our self-absorption and apathy can fail. Even setting aside some of the most important questions—like how structural barriers in the media filter out certain kinds of reporting,[7] how the global interests of the United States and other powerful countries determine what fits into and what is excluded from the agenda of international human rights,[8] and how government policy can be insulated against kindled public emotion—even setting all this aside, the range of obstacles can be daunting. John Conroy, for instance, in his book *Unspeakable Acts, Ordinary People* (2000), lists nine typical rejoinders by democratic societies to accusations that they have committed torture: flatly denying it; admitting it but minimizing the abuse; disparaging the victims as criminals or terrorists; justifying it through appeal to emergency circumstances; condemning as corrupt, untrustworthy, or foreign those organizations exposing the abuse; insisting that violations are being dealt with or are a matter of the past; shifting the blame to "a few bad apples"; mitigating the torture by comparing it to even more extreme torture elsewhere; and finally dismissing it by claiming that those tortured will soon "get over it."[9]

Even in the absence of effective counter-representations by perpetrators and sponsors, there are a range of reasons why stories of atrocity fail to move global bystanders to intervene. In *Denial and Acknowledgment,* Stanley Cohen enumerates some of the psychological causes of passivity in response to cries for help: diffusion of responsibility (he points to the infamous 1964 incident in which a young woman named Kitty Genovese was murdered while an entire New York neighborhood watched and listened, each person assuming that someone else would take action); inability to conceive of an effective intervention; inhibition due to uncertainty or complexity of knowledge; inability to identify with strangers; and compassion fatigue.[10]

Journalist Peter Maass, who reported on the war in Bosnia in the early 1990s, has written of the disillusionment that results from the international community's persisting indifference to accounts and images of suffering. "This is when you start to feel the spiritual sickness . . . if you sense futility, if you can no longer look a Bosnian in the eye and say, in honesty, that the reason the world doesn't react is because it doesn't know what's happening or doesn't understand. When you conclude that the world does know, and does understand, and still doesn't react, your time is up."[11]

The Ethics of Humanitarian and Human Rights Work as a Career

Here, too, the issue is defined by two opposing poles. In the years I spent interviewing people for this book, I met many who had sacrificed their health, financial status, and emotional well-being because they could not stand by and watch as catastrophes unfolded around them, because they felt they had to do something. Many risked their lives, and some had colleagues who died on mission. But just as human rights as a moral concept has come under increasing pressure and scrutiny in recent years, so have the motivations of such individuals.

In *The Road to Hell,* a scathing critique of the effects of foreign aid, former aid worker Michael Maren recalls his first meeting with fellow volunteers in the Peace Corps. Everybody was asked to explain his or her reason for volunteering; nearly everybody said they wanted to help people. Maren confesses to a more self-centered reason—the lure of exotic adventure—but as critical as he is of his own motives, it is the desire to help others that he condemns most harshly. "It was easy to presume that people need our help," he writes. "The starving African exists as a point in space from which we measure our own wealth, success, and prosperity, a darkness against which we can view our own cultural triumphs. And he serves as a handy object of our charity. He is evidence that we have been blessed, and we have an obligation to spread that blessing. The belief that we can help is an affirmation of our own worth in the grand scheme of things."[12]

Maren's characterizations and rhetoric have been criticized by some as excessive, but his charge remains important and highlights a basic impasse in moral evaluation. As Elliot Sober and David Wilson explain in their study of altruism, whether we judge human actions to be intrinsically selfish or altruistic is a matter of irreconcilable world views.[13] The school of thought dubbed *psychological egoism* argues that all of the actions we undertake, even ostensibly altruistic ones, are ultimately self-promoting—if only because they affirm our own worth. *Psychological altruism*, by contrast, argues that self-interest cannot account for all our actions. It dismisses the argument from egoism as "unfalsifiable." In other words, any motive can be re-described to sound selfish, which means that no conceivable evidence can be offered to challenge the validity of psychological egoism. This, in turn, makes psychological egoism seem less like a theory of human behavior, and more like an a priori moral worldview. So what are we to make of psychological egoism and the force of claims, like Maren's, that human rights work is ultimately selfish?

What Difference Does Humanitarian and Human Rights Work Make?

It is difficult to measure the difference such work makes because, as with altruism, every example can be analyzed from two fundamentally irreconcilable standpoints: in this case, from a stance that is subjective (individual, personalized) and one that is objective (depersonalized, statistical, aggregate).

The first thing to measure is intended consequences. How are we to value small benefits against great harms—or, rather, the limited scope of what we can accomplish against the seemingly limitless scope of urgent needs? For the detainee released or the refugee resettled, the value of the organizations and norms that make rescue possible can be immeasurable. From an objective stance, however, the value is not only measurable but, for some critics, dubious. One issue here is the scarce-resources dilemma and the problem of choice: that is, thousands must be abandoned to make possible the concentration of resources needed to rescue a small number of chosen individuals. And, as many relief workers have observed, the choice is often determined by the need to generate donor support through media attention. In other words, many organizations are pressured into concentrating their efforts on high-visibility crises that suit Western tastes, even when they believe it is a misuse of aid resources.[14] Former president of Médecins Sans Frontières (MSF) Rony Brauman points to the Western response to the 2004 Asian tsunami as a classic instance of the misapplication of aid resources. It happened near Christmas, so people gave generously, even though the money was not needed and in fact the crowding of NGOs (nongovernmental organizations) on the ground only complicated recovery efforts. David Kennedy, discussing human rights violations, argues that even when help is well targeted it can sometimes become part of a larger statistical problem: "Human rights remedies, even when successful, treat the symptoms rather than the illness, and this allows the illness not only to fester, but to seem like health itself. . . . Even where victims are recompensed or violations avoided, the distributions of power and wealth which produced the violation may well come to seem more legitimate as they seek other avenues of expression."[15]

The second category to measure, as Kennedy's criticism

reveals, is unintended consequences. How do we weigh
the unforeseen and often unforeseeable negative results
of our humanitarian interventions? The aftermath of the
Rwandan genocide is often pointed to as evidence of the
danger of simple good intentions in complex crises. Mary
Anderson describes what happened when the murderous
Hutu regime was defeated: "As refugees poured from
Rwanda into eastern Zaire and the humanitarian assistance
community wished to preserve life in this unhealthy setting, international aid workers report that the circumstances seemed to be an 'aid provider's dream.' Whole villages arrived together with leadership structures intact so
that early decisions about how to allocate and distribute
food seemed easy." But this apparent order belied an in-
vidious reality: "It is now well known that the 'leadership'
was the Hutu militia who had committed the genocide in
Rwanda. They were able to use the resources provided by
international humanitarian aid to control civilian populations and to rearm and prepare for a return battle in
Rwanda."[16] From a subjective stance, the defense of the
humanitarian endeavor here depends upon the urgent
moral priority of motivation. To be able to help at all, we
have to be the sort of people who would help even in this
case, who would be likely to be thus misguided. We must
continue to take such risks because we are driven by mo-

tives it would be wrong to lose. As Brauman writes, the "injunction to remain close to people in distress and to try to relieve their suffering without discrimination cannot be relativized."[17] From an objective stance, however, this is not a convincing set of claims. If it is true that your good intentions cause more harm than good, we would all be better off if you abandoned them.

The more people I interviewed for this book, the heavier the weight of negating claims like these became. In what other ways can humanitarian aid amplify crises? To the militarization of refugee camps and safety zones, already discussed, MSF researcher Fiona Terry adds this list: it can provide a tool for controlling the movement of populations (in Bosnia, for instance, policies of ethnic expulsion were furthered by evacuation assistance and the lure of humanitarian aid); it can contribute to war economies (directly, through taxes and fees paid to local governments, and indirectly, through theft of supplies); and it can bestow legitimacy on aggressive governments and movements (directly, by cooperating with them in the media spotlight, and indirectly, by helping them fulfill their social obligations to their people).[18] One delegate from the International Committee of the Red Cross gave me a more chilling example, expressing his fear that ICRC efforts to trace the disappeared in one country may have led to their executions. "The authorities didn't want to recognize that they were detaining people illegally," he said. "They preferred to kill them."

Leaving aside the terrible problem of unintended consequences and inadvertent complicity does little to help. Attempts to measure the success or failure of humanitarian work are, *by the very nature of the work,* always an experience in loss. It doesn't matter how many people are saved—every time it is a failure; every time there are the unsaved. But as worker after worker insisted to me, to respond cynically is a mistake. Brauman put it this way when I asked him what hopes drive his work: "We're not preparing for any radiant or bright future." Humanitarian action is always defined by ethical dilemmas, and sometimes "by having to act but having nothing but bad choices available. For me as a doctor this is a banal fact. A surgery can be a way of hurting and every drug is also a poison. It is no different for humanitarian action writ large. We cannot control that. We can only focus on what we do now, in the present, with those in front of us. Our success can only be in the moment."

As Brauman once said elsewhere in response to a question about the failures of humanitarian work: "When one speaks of a failure, one implies that there could be success. I have a hard time imagining what a humanitarian success would be in situations where violence is itself the sign of failure. As humanitarians we inscribe ourselves in failure."[19] It is in understandings like these, I will argue, that we might very well find our best hope.

Senegalese writer Boubacar Boris Diop told me a story about Rwanda. Toward the end of the hundred-day geno-cide in 1994, when forces of the Rwandan Patriotic Front (RPF) began an advance that drove the génocidaires out of the country, they encountered dogs. The dogs were unusu-ally large and fierce, having fed well on the heaps of corpses choking the roadways. RPF soldiers, sickened by this final indignity, and hoping to preserve as much as possible of the dead for proper burial, began to shoot the dogs. Immediately, animal rights groups in London launched a protest to protect the dogs.

Diop's story is, in essence, a story about failing to be-come a story. By some counts, 10,000 people a day were killed in the Rwandan genocide—but somehow the story didn't take hold in the international imagination. French president François Mitterrand is reported to have said: "In those countries, genocide is not very important."[1] General Roméo Dallaire, the force commander of the UN assistance mission to Rwanda during the genocide, recalls a conversation with an American staffer engaged in a planning exercise: the staffer had calculated that it would "take the deaths of 85,000 Rwandans to justify the risking of the life of one American soldier."[2] And Diop himself confesses: "Honesty compels me to admit that the Rwandan tragedy provoked, if possible, even less interest in Africa than in the rest of the world."[3] The Africa Cup soccer matches, he recalls, monopolized his attention as the killings began.

But what makes Diop's story so interesting is how interesting a story it is, how quickly it compels attention and how hard it is to forget. That is to say, the story about the failed story is itself a satisfying story that serves important cultural purposes. The world's failure to recognize the genocide, its failure to value the lives of Africans, has, if anything, become a more potent and vivid story in the West than the genocide itself ever could be. We are culpable, and it feels good to be culpable. It assures us that we are good people, because we are the kind of people who feel bad about these sorts of things. And we're proud because we aren't ashamed to admit it—as Bill Clinton did for us all, four years after the height of the genocide, in his

famous apology to the Rwandan people during a visit that
didn't take him beyond the Kigali airport.

■■■■■ This chapter is about the stories that have been
made out of the Rwandan genocide. More generally, as a
frame for all the chapters that follow, it is about how we
make stories (pleas, arguments, cases, testimonies, memoirs, novels) out of catastrophic violence, out of events
that by their very nature resist coherent representation.
What purposes do they serve, public and private? How
does the storytelling affect the audience, the storyteller,
and those who have been made into a story? When are stories effective in moving their audiences—moving them not
only to feel, but to act in response to the moral claims of a
narrative? And when do they fail?

Rwanda begins as a failure of stories. Augustin
Nzigamsabo, a teacher from Butare, survived a machete
attack by throwing himself into the Kanyaro River. "I cannot find the words to describe how I felt," he said, trem-
bling, in his testimony to the London-based organization
African Rights. Fortunata Ngirabatware was brutally assaulted by the Hutu militia known as the Interahamwe.
She survived, but was unable to speak for three weeks.

Three more weeks later, also giving testimony to African
Rights, she could not speak without a stammer.[4] Stephen
Smith, of American RadioWorks, recalls interviewing the
mother of several murdered children; she physically col-
lapsed shortly after the interview began and was unable to
continue. Grace Munyakazi-Umutoni, an exiled Rwandan,
told a typical story when she spoke to me about a young
cousin who has been silent since the genocide.

The silence of deep shock is betrayed by—but also bears
a structural psychic relationship to—the silence of "bystander's avoidance," the hush attendant upon the very human desire to look away. But the failure of Rwanda as a
story is not just a matter of the unrepresentability of survivors' trauma or of the Western world's wish to avoid seeing things that could be left alone, once truly seen, only at
the cost of its righteous self-conception. It is also, and perhaps more fundamentally, a matter of racism. Journalist
Philip Gourevitch comments: "There was a study done.
During the first thirty days of the genocide, in the American print media virtually no Rwandans, no Rwandan civilians, were identified by name. So you had a faceless, anonymous mass of Africans. And what do Africans do in the
American press? They die of miserable things."[5]

The problem of racial frames is exacerbated in the case

of Rwanda, for two reasons. First, because confessing to it is self-serving, because the repetitive identification of race-guilt here functions simultaneously as a form of self-flagellation that reminds Americans of their moral excellence and as a vivid displacement of the guilt owed, so to speak, closer to home. Second, and more importantly for the purposes of this chapter, because in the anglophone world virtually all of the genocide's story-tellers are outsiders. Whether benevolent or self-serving, they are speaking for Rwanda, not from it. "Rwandans have to suffer through the images created by the media," Diop said to me. "It is impossible for them to give a proper answer to those images." As Africans, he said, "we simply have to refuse or accept the images that are sent to us"—and many, he concluded, "are resigned to accepting those images."[6]

The moral problem of this sort of traumatic ventriloquism is bounded by two opposing questions that will, in one way or another, provide a frame for each of the sections that follow: Do I have the right to talk about this? And, do I have the right *not* to talk about this? It is bounded, in other words, by the poles of entitlement (What gives me the moral authority to tell this story? How can I prove my authenticity to my readers?) and obligation

(How much of myself am I required to give to this story? What is my duty, and when am I free of it?).

Let's begin with a study in contrasts.

In 1996 at the Fest'Africa, a celebration of African literature held in Lille, France, a group of African authors made a public declaration against the military dictatorship of Sani Abacha for his execution of Nigerian writer Ken Saro-Wiwa the previous year. According to Diop, those involved in the action felt driven to express their outrage even as they knew "their pens were powerless to stop the killers."[7] What were the moral obligations of artists and authors, and what could they do to make a difference? Over the next several months the writers' "increasingly urgent desire to make themselves heard"[8] generated "Writing by Duty of Memory," a project that sent ten authors to Rwanda to find some way to tell the story of the war and the genocide it had catalyzed.

Diop was part of that group. He had written about Rwanda before, if only briefly, to try "to relieve his conscience." But as an African intellectual and journalist, he told me, he felt great shame for having taken so long to devote himself fully to representing the genocide. During the

"Duty of Memory" project, Diop and his group spent time
with survivors and orphans and spoke with some of the
prisoners accused of acts of genocide. He did not talk
about the former but described several encounters with
the latter, including a meeting with a group who told him
how they had eaten parts of their victims and drunk their
blood and, more disturbingly because it inspired his pity, a
visit to the interrogation of a génocidaire whose ears had
been cut off when he was captured. "He was an execu-
tioner, yet he looked pitiful."

Diop and the other project participants were not tour-
ists of misery, like so many of the well-intentioned Westerners who now visit Rwanda (Munyakazi-Umutoni told
me straightforwardly that the genocide has been "great"
for tourism). The experience for these writers was not a
matter of acquiring moral capital but a matter of paying
debts; and, if anything, the work only amplified their sense
of their obligations. Chadian author Koulsy Lamko, Diop
said, felt he had to stay in Rwanda, felt writing one book
(*La phalène des collines* [The Moth of the Hills]) was not
enough. He remained for several years in "rather precarious conditions" because he felt he had no right to leave;
afterward he created a Center for the Arts at the University of Butare, intended as "a place of discussion to help
the healing of Rwandans." When pressed, Diop confessed

to suffering stress-related illnesses when writing about Rwanda after his time there, and again even later, when composing the preface to Yolande Mukagasana's book of witness accounts, *Les blessures du silence* (The Wounds of Silence). "For a year or two after I wrote the preface," he said, "I had to stop reading about Rwanda. I created a bookstore at the information center on Rwanda, in Dakar, close to where I live, but I could not go there and open a book for a long time. I started again a few weeks ago but I no longer read the testimonies of the victims. I only read the work explaining what happened."

Some of the survivors Diop met in Rwanda begged him: "Please don't turn what we tell you into novels."[9] They were anxious about the kind of stories being told, about being turned into stories. "People wanted to remain human beings and not become characters," he said. "Literature can make things more beautiful and more acceptable," he added. "I think the people we met feared this." Diop stayed two months and earned, he believes, the trust of those he met. "After going to Rwanda, listening to the stories of the survivors, seeing remains and smelling terrible odors, it would be a disgrace to return to Senegal and roll up my sleeves ready to tell everyone how great a writer I was." He was deeply suspicious of the project of writing in this circumstance, in particular of the prom-

ise of understanding implicit in the effort. "Understanding
helps you go beyond things," he said. "[It] gives you a feeling of intellectual satisfaction." Writing like this, Diop felt,
would be a betrayal. He wanted to write differently, humbly.

The book he finally completed, *Murambi: Le livre des
ossements* (Murambi: The Book of Bones), has been translated into multiple languages, including English; at the
Zimbabwe International Book Fair, it was designated one
of the 100 most important African books of the twentieth
century. Even so, Diop has had difficulty with his book in
much of Africa: "Africans are used to such atrocities. We
have an alienated conscience that makes us believe we're
guilty. We, as African intellectuals, have a self-persuaded
feeling of inferiority—I sadly must acknowledge it." When
Diop first approached a US publisher, the reaction was
equally disheartening: he says he was told that Rwanda
was old news, that it was too complicated. The reaction
was much the same when a friend of his offered a documentary on Rwanda to French television. "They said to
him, 'No, we do not want to show an event that is too far
in the past, and that people have forgotten.'"

Julian Pierce's *Speak Rwanda* is another of the rare novels about the Rwandan genocide that is available in English. (I do not count books like Elmore Leonard's *Pagan
Babies*, where the genocide is used as a spicy backdrop.)
Speak Rwanda is a sometimes awkward, sometimes power-

ful novel. Among other things, it abounds in talk of magic
amulets, initiation spears, and exotic diets (Tutsi women,
we are told in the opening lines, shame their men if they
eat meat). It is as if Pierce collected as many attention-
grabbing details as possible and foregrounded them
throughout the novel for their cash value, so to speak. His
characters, as one review put it, "seem more emblems
than individuals."[10] But the novel is nevertheless authentic—the back cover insists as much in its short, needy bio:
"Julian R. Pierce is an American who has worked and traveled throughout Africa, where he maintains close ties with
friends and loved ones in Rwanda."

Anxious bio notwithstanding, *Speak Rwanda* is not the
book I look to for an example of a sharp, illuminating
contrast with Diop's *Murambi*. For that, I turn to *A Sunday
at the Pool in Kigali*, by French-Canadian author Gil
Courtemanche. *A Sunday at the Pool in Kigali* is the most
successful fiction about the genocide to be translated and
published in English. It is also the *most* authentic: as
Courtemanche proudly says, he took real people, used
their real names, and turned them into characters in a novel.

Here is the climax of the story Courtemanche has
made out of the Rwandan genocide. Gentille, a beautiful
young waitress, is imprisoned in the home of one of the

génocidaires because she looks like a Tutsi. She is gang-raped for a week. Her reaction is astonishing and morally wrenching, but before I describe it, along with Diop's reaction when asked about the book, let me backtrack.

The character of Gentille is based on a waitress who worked at the Hôtel des Mille Collines in Kigali, a beautiful woman whom Courtemanche was too shy to talk to. In the novel, the protagonist, an aging French-Canadian journalist like Courtemanche, talks to her, makes her have orgasms by speaking to her in French, and marries her. Then she is captured.

To backtrack once more. According to a review in the Canadian newspaper *La Presse, A Sunday at the Pool in Kigali* is "the novel of the year . . . a fresco with humanist accents which could easily find a place next to the works of Albert Camus and Graham Greene."[11] It won the 2001 Canadian Prix des Libraires for outstanding book of the year, has been sold in more than a dozen countries, and is being made into a film by Montreal-based Lyla Films.

To return to the novel, and to Gentille's reaction to the repeated gang-rapes. She is certain she's going to be killed when the men are done with her; she keeps a diary so somebody will hear her story. One of the great regrets she expresses is that her rapists aren't very good lovers. "Since I'm going to die, I'd rather my rapist remind me of my husband and give me pleasure. I know it's ridiculous.

This time he was in less of a hurry and pawed my breasts
and my buttocks. Not a single memory came back. I'm
ashamed not to want to resist, but I still want to live." And
later: "Bernard, I'm speaking to you and I see you listening. I know you don't hold it against me that I've looked
for pleasure in my pain. But I haven't been able to guide
them to the paths I discovered with you. They don't hear
me. . . . If I can't get any pleasure from this slow walk toward death, I might as well run out into the sun and die
from one machete slash."[12]

In the end, the tragic lack of pleasure in her rapes
only reminds her of how wonderful a lover the French-
Canadian journalist was: "Bernard, why did you have me
discover what a mysterious, secret garden the body is, a
garden for exploring endlessly without ever finding the beginning or the end? Why did you teach me desire, and also
the ecstasy of creating the other's climax? A few days ago I
was a thousand points of pleasure, a thousand musical
notes transformed into a hymn by your fingers, your lips,
your tongue."[13]

In the novel she is not finally murdered. She is mutilated
and abandoned but survives. Yet she dies soon after the
genocide from an AIDS-related infection, alone, because
she has become an "ugly thing" and does not want to be
seen.[14] The real Gentille disappeared in the genocide.

A review in the Australian newspaper The Age calls the

book "a gentle love story."[15] Here's a typical moment from the novel:

> "Gentille, d'you know when I fell in love with you?"
>
> "The night you came and drove me home?"
>
> "No, the first morning. It was six o'clock and you'd just started your internship. I'd asked for eggs turned over, but they weren't. With bacon, but I ended up with ham. But all I could see were your breasts almost cutting through your starched blouse and your behind that must have been shaped by a genius of a sculptor."[16]

The review in *The Age* briefly mentions the "frosty" response from "politically correct women writers." Courtemanche dismisses the criticism thus: "They ask, 'How come a white man can write about the sexual life of a black woman?' But curiously enough, the black women I met in Rwanda come back and say, 'Thanks for writing that.' They whisper in my ear because they wouldn't like their husbands to hear."

After Diop told me the story of the scavenging dogs, I thought of Courtemanche's book and asked him about it. "I was not interested in reading it," Diop explained. "It is like the man is saying: This is the genocide. And *this* is Gil Courtemanche." For this very reason, ICRC delegates—

who risked their lives to stay in Rwanda and help when all others fled—are reluctant to talk about their experiences, and even more reluctant to have their stories shared publicly. ICRC delegate Jean-François Sangsue was frankly suspicious of my project when I asked him about his work during the genocide: "The worst thing to be done, and the least respectful attitude, would be to talk about ICRC delegates instead of trying to keep in mind what the Rwandan people went through and what they live with now."

In Courtemanche's story, by contrast, just as with Diop's story of the dogs, the genocide becomes primarily an occasion for whites to fantasize about themselves—in this case, not moral self-congratulation but rather sexual self-comforting through the inversion of racist stereotypes: black women whisper secretly in the ears of the white man, who is more desirable, and more free in his desire, than hapless black cuckolds. The aging French-Canadian journalist does admit to himself that he is not as robust as a young African man—he is more mind than body, so to speak—but he knows he can beat them in the game of love anyway because he is smart about the body and its pleasures.

Genocide and war, after all, are all about our power over other people's bodies. Indeed, by some accounts part of the initial force that swept young Hutu men to the roadblocks was the promise of rape, the promise of unre-

stricted access to and control over women's bodies (rape
was "a weapon of war," writes African Rights, and women
were "the spoils of genocide").[17] The genocide was, at least
in part, a perceived opportunity for self-extension, for real-
izing a vision of a powerful, amplified self. The imagined
or hypothesized adventure, for writers like Courtemanche,
is not entirely different. The genocide functions almost
like a mirror, allowing the observer to gaze upon himself,
to see how he has acquired new depth and meaning by
encountering tragedy, to see how he has proven himself.
This is so, according to some, for all of us. In 1994 the
New York Times quoted a British military psychiatrist in
Rwanda as saying, "A fascination with death has created
a voyeurism among Westerners here—the relief agencies,
the United Nations and the journalists." The *Times* reporter continued: "Western visitors regularly tour massacre sites where bodies are rotting and still unburied. Visiting
diplomats have driven for hours to see bodies washed up in
the eddies of the Akagera River on the Tanzanian border."[18] Medical anthropologists Arthur and Joan Kleinman
link these comments to "the more ominous aspects of
globalization, such as the commercialization of suffering,
the commodification of experiences of atrocity and abuse,
and the pornographic uses of degradation."[19]

    Again, race is a key element here—references to Joseph

Conrad's *Heart of Darkness* abound in Western representations of the genocide, self-consciously reproducing the notion of Africa as a site of grim self-discovery for white
men.[20] I don't mean to insist, however, that racism is necessarily the only motivator, that it alone is what has attracted
people to the genocide. Because violence at that scale trig-
gers so many cognitive resistances, because its disorganiza-
tion makes it so difficult to pack it into the standard narrative forms we use for parceling knowledge of our worlds,
we can be inclined to retreat into easy, familiar methods of
regulating experience. For many, racism can therefore begin to function as an almost indispensable enabling device,
a useful and well-practiced response for psychically organizing the unorganizable. Many turn it into a personal adventure framed by familiar racial fantasies because, in part
at least, they don't know where else to start.

██████████ Many characters are portrayed with contempt in
Courtemanche's novel, but few with such dismissive ridi-
cule as UN General Dallaire. Courtemanche, who was
in Paris when the killings began, describes Dallaire as "ap-
prehensive, ineloquent and naïve, like Canada." Dallaire is
ignorant of war, the world, and particularly Africa. He
thinks the massacres with which the genocide begins are

mere "misconduct." He thinks ethnic cleansing is "a problem between Rwandans."[21] At the end of the novel, in
what Courtemanche surely means for the reader to experience as a satisfying, righteous moment, a Rwandan being sheltered at the Mille Collines spits on Dallaire's shoes
and says, "Shut up. You're pathetic. They killed ten of
your own soldiers and even then you didn't react."[22]
Courtemanche even makes fun of Dallaire for having a
moustache.[23]

   Others have been no less harsh in their judgment. On
December 6, 1997, the Belgian senate released a report
from a commission of inquiry on Rwanda calling Dallaire's
conduct ineffective and unprofessional. At a public conference in Rwanda, Belgian senator Alain Destexhe went
further, blaming Dallaire for failing to rescue ten Belgian
soldiers who were murdered in the initial hours of the
genocide, accusing him of ignoring their widows, and arguing that he had obeyed criminal orders from the UN De-
partment of Peacekeeping Operations (DPKO). But it is
Dallaire himself who has been the harshest judge. He has
publicly apologized to the Rwandan people for—in his
words—failing them, and has attempted suicide.

   When I met Dallaire it was more than a decade after the
genocide, when he had just been appointed to the Canadian senate. Belated public acknowledgment of the impos-

sibility of his situation, together with an increasing intoler-
ance for those who comfortably judged from a distance
how he should have acted during one of the fastest killing sprees of the twentieth century, had created a radically new story of the man. Nick Nolte represented him
with frustrated dignity in the film *Hotel Rwanda,* and an
award-winning documentary film by Peter Raymont depicted him as a hero who had foreseen the genocide and
warned the international community, only to be ignored
and finally abandoned, left in the middle of the slaughter
with a handful of troops inadequately equipped even for
self-defense. His book *Shake Hands with the Devil* had been
awarded Canada's Governor General's Literary Award for
Non-Fiction in 2004; he had been made an Officer of the
Order of Canada; and he had received the Aegis Trust Reward "for altruism, resourcefulness and bravery in pre-
serving the value of human life." Harvard University had
designated him a Human Rights Policy Fellow, and the International Rescue Committee had given him its Distin-
guished Humanitarian Award. In a speech at the award ceremony in 2004, UN secretary general Kofi Annan said:
"While the genocide showed us the very worst of humanity, Roméo showed us some of the very best. He has paid a
terrible price for that, in terms of personal distress and
self-doubt. But even that is tribute to his deep humanity. As

soldier, peacekeeper and humanitarian, and above all as a
fine example of what it should mean to be a human being,
he richly deserves tonight's recognition and award."[24]

There's a cruder version of the reasons for this recognition: in a time of human rights chic, Dallaire is a celebrity for witnessing genocide. "I think it's reflective of how
superficial the Western world is," he said when I asked him
about this. "It needs something tangible, visible, and I'm
filling a certain role there. As long as it keeps the Rwandan
genocide alive, I'll go with it. It's a tool. And I'm going to
maximize that tool to help the Rwandans as much as I can.
But I find that it's reflective of our inability to grasp difficult things for what they are." He continued: "A long time
ago I promised I would do whatever I could to keep the
genocide alive." If becoming a story is part of it, as either
hero or villain, "that's fine."

For Dallaire, returning to Rwanda again and again—being that story for us, in interviews and talks and writings—
is like unsuturing a wound each time. He recalls how painful it was to give testimony at the International Criminal
Tribunal for Rwanda, how telling the story was like "reliv-
ing it." Here is a sample of his testimony for the prosecution, in response to a question about what he saw at the
roadblocks. It begins tentatively, in the passive, but quickly
gains momentum:

Oh, they were all civilian. I don't remember a uni-
formed person. And there were babies and pregnant
women, babies, children, elderly. Some of the sites—
well, at a number of the sites mutilation was done on
men, and you could see by the layout of the women
and so on that rape and then mutilation had happened.

Here the prosecutor presses for more details about the female corpses.

Well, I'm not—I can't say it was a standard operating
procedure by the extremists as such, but we could
notice on many sites, sometimes very fresh—that is,
I am speaking of my observers and myself—that
young girls, young women, would be laid out with
their dresses over their heads, their legs spread and
bent. You could see what seemed to be semen dry-
ing or dried. And it all indicated to me that these
women were raped. And then a variety of material
were crushed or implanted into their vaginas; their
breasts were cut off, and the faces were, in many
cases, still the eyes were open and there was like a
face that seemed horrified or something. They all laid
on their backs. So there were some men that were

mutilated also, their genitals and the like. A number
of them were—women had their breasts cut off or
their stomach open.

Here the prosecution presses for more: How much was
there?

It got to the point that we, in fact, would put someone in front of our vehicles to walk because whenever you saw a rag on the road or something, you
were never sure whether you were rolling over a
corpse or not, and often it was a corpse. In fact, it
made it quite difficult at times to be able to take
some of these roads because you had to take the decision whether you roll over the corpses, or have to
go back and find another route and so on.[25]

"I've got six or seven years of therapy behind me, and
that's done next to nothing," he told me later. "The traumatic memory will never diminish. You try to build a pros-
thesis to control it. What you hope is through medication
and therapy. . . ." He stopped here. "None of the stuff ever
disappears. It's a matter of avoiding scenarios that trigger
things." Even writing a book—for literary critics, the classic example of therapeutic self-realization—provided no
release. "The more and more we got into it, the more it

dragged us into hell." One of the people working with him on the book committed suicide in the process. "There is nothing positive in this in any way, shape, or form. It's just a goddamn slugfest with yourself." He still blames himself for the dead.

Dallaire is a broken man. But that breaking is also what sustains him; it is also, now, the meaning of his life. He cannot change his choices and cannot redeem the dead. But he can use the time that remains to him to undo one harm of the genocide, to be effective against at least one of its crimes: that is, the deliberate elimination of speech.

The Rwandan genocide worked so well because it directly assaulted communication: key public voices (journalists, activists, opposition politicians) were targeted for execution, domestic telephone lines in Kigali were cut, and curfews and roadblocks prevented public protests. When the prefect of Butare effectively shut down violence before it began, by traveling freely through the area and speaking publicly and privately to military and civilian groups alike, he was murdered.[26] "Cutting communications served several purposes," African Rights sums up. "It allowed the killers to restrict the movements of their targeted victims, to control the flow of news to the population, and to confuse and mislead the outside world, so that they could carry on the killing undisturbed."[27]

The genocide was, in key ways, a language war. The government worked hard both to silence its opponents and victims and to fill the void it created with noise—in other words, to replace accurate and clear language with lies. The role of the Rwandan media, the radio in particular, has been publicized by the famous "Media Trial" at the International Criminal Tribunal for Rwanda (ICTR), where two media executives were sentenced to life imprisonment and a third to twenty-seven years for using the media to incite genocide. As Judge Navanethem Pillay put it in her judgment: "You were fully aware of the power of words. . . . Without a firearm, machete, or any physical weapon, you caused the deaths of thousands of innocent civilians."[28]

Génocidaires manipulated the media not only to incite violence but also to control how outsiders (who could intervene) perceived events in Rwanda. They found unexpected allies. In the "contest to out-describe" their dwindling targets,[29] the government continually used language that deflected, distorted, and minimized agency and responsibility. Dr. Casimir Bizimungu, minister of health for the self-proclaimed interim government during the genocide, deplored the "massacres" that were the result of "inter-ethnic" tension and RPF aggression, and referred dismissively to "the theory of 'genocide.'"[30] Col. Marcel Gatsinzi explained the "massacres" by the presence of "bandits" and "undisciplined troops" "here and there."[31] At a press conference in Nairobi, minister of commerce Justin Mugenzi advocated the view that the killings were the organic result of unplanned, "uncontrollable," "popular anger" over the assassination of Rwanda's president; and chairman of the MRND Matthieu Ngirumpatse insisted "people killed on their own, without any authority."[32] Théodore Sindikubwabo, president of the interim government, spoke of the "activism" of a "resistance movement by the youth and the whole population against foreign aggression."[33] On German television, the minister of foreign affairs, Jérôme Bicumumpaka, explained that "the Tutsis and Hutus have massacred each other to an equal extent," and added chillingly that ICRC death tolls were "grossly exaggerated." "It can't count the number of wounded and dead or even estimate them. How could it? There are no witnesses to give evidence."[34]

The foreign media played their part, repeatedly talking not about genocide but about "tribal violence," "anarchy," and the "ancient tribal feud."[35] So did the son of accused génocidaire Pastor Elizaphan Ntakirutimana: speaking with Philip Gourevitch before his father's arrest, he attributed the killings only to "chaos, chaos, chaos."[36] Military spokesmen for France, which had historical ties to the Hutu majority government, supported the blame-negating notion

of a "two-way genocide," and Filip Reynthens, a leading
Belgian authority on Rwanda, told the *New York Times:*
"It's not a story of good guys and bad guys. It's a story of
bad guys. Period."[37] The achingly disingenuous response
of the United States, keen to avoid its responsibilities under the Genocide Convention of 1948, is now notorious
(Samantha Power's book *A Problem from Hell* tracks carefully the shameful rhetorical squirming of the Clinton administration). Here is Christine Shelly, the State Depart-
ment spokesperson, two months into the genocide,
responding to reporters and trying to stick to the administration's official formulation that Rwanda was experiencing "acts of genocide" rather than "genocide":

Q: *So you say genocide happens when certain acts happen, and you
say that those acts have happened in Rwanda. So why can't you
say that genocide has happened?*

A: *Because, Alan, there is a reason for the selection of words that we
have made, and I have—perhaps I have—I'm not a lawyer. I don't
approach this from the international legal and scholarly point of
view. We try, as best as we can, to accurately reflect a description
in particularly addressing that issue. It's—the issue is out there.
People have obviously been looking at it.*[38]

François Karera, former prefect of Greater Kigali, put the
argument against the word "genocide" more directly: "You

cannot use that word 'genocide' because there are numerous [Tutsis] surviving."[39]

The story told by Spéciose Mukayiraba about the death of her husband, human rights activist Fidèle Kanyabugoyi, stands as a tragic paradigm both for the transparent fabrications used to justify the killing and for the final triumph of silence:

> I was covered by dead bodies. But my husband, who was lying slightly in front of me, was not. I saw the interahamwe approach him and ask him for money. He looked in his coat pocket, obviously forgetting that all his money had already been taken from him by other militia. Then they asked him whether he had celebrated the President's death. He replied no. They also wanted to know whether he had ever participated in demonstrations and he said no. Suddenly they hit him with a machete. I did not dare look closely because I could not let them see that I was not dead. I heard Fidèle whispering, his voice getting more and more feeble. He was talking about how we had been assembled there and how we were being treated. It was as if he was relating a report to a human rights organization. As I was listening to Fidèle, an interahamwe stepped on my chest. . . . I played dead in spite of the excruciating pain.[40]

For many, it was as if the world had become deaf to their cries. Jean-Paul Biramvu recalls when Belgian troops made the decision to pull out. Thousands had gathered at the Ecole Technique Officielle in Kicukiro, believing that the nearby troops would protect them:

> The Belgians left around 2:00 P.M. They had not told us anything. They tried to sneak away. But some of us saw them leave, hurriedly grabbing their belongings. There were foreigners amongst us, and they had not even said anything to them. We could not believe what they were doing—just abandoning us when they knew the place was surrounded by killers. They jumped into their cars very suddenly and sped away. It still did not dawn on us that they were actually leaving. With thousands of unarmed refugees surrounded by the Presidential Guards and the interahamwe, such a thought was unthinkable. . . . In desperation, some of the young men threw themselves on the road to prevent them from leaving us. Some of the Belgian soldiers took out grenades. They did not throw them into the crowd but their action frightened everyone and people moved back from the road. Some of us who had cars wanted to jump into their cars and to run after the Belgian sol-

diers. . . . As soon as the Belgian soldiers were out of the gate, the firing started.

At one point, the militia herded the refugees together on the road, as a way of organizing the killing that would follow. Biramvu remembers sitting on the road when a group of UN soldiers drove by. "Although we were surrounded," he said, "we cried out to them, saying: 'Save us, save us!' But they just passed on."[41]

These were Dallaire's troops. So it is to this place that Dallaire continually returns. He quite explicitly sees his life as a mission to make sure we hear those voices—the reports on dying breaths, the pleas of the crowds—and to replace the quiet of the murdered with clear, unrelenting language. Keeping the talking going was then, and remains now, Dallaire's best and perhaps only way to counter the violence and its legacy.

Indeed, one of the most striking things about his book is how fixated it is on acts of language. Many readers, no doubt, will be surprised by his relative reticence about the details of the killings and, by contrast, his almost startling abundance of details about paperwork. On page after page he focuses on the action he took, or tried to take, through language: negotiations, code cables, situation reports, letters, press conferences, prayers, meetings, and even (repeatedly) accounts of efforts to maintain adequate supplies of pencils and paper. It is an exhausting record of Dallaire's efforts to decelerate violence through unceasing talk. As things got worse, he told me, "the only solution that I saw was more, just meeting people more and more." It is difficult to get Dallaire to say anything positive about his work in Rwanda, but when pressed he told me he remained proud of two things: that he was able to be a "conduit" for moderates, "to keep those lines of communications open"; and that he was able to get the media to tell the story. "It was a constant exercise in trying to keep communications going," he summed up, "because that's your mission."

As the Western world's primary witness, Dallaire is given many chances to speak: films, books, lectures, courtroom testimony. But as much as he speaks, he is also spoken. Like the genocide itself, he is used as material. This is a key problematic for both the witness and the survivor as categories: to control how the story is told, you must surrender your rights to control the story. Dallaire is made into a text by all around him, for purposes that help him realize his deep commitments but that also violate them. For instance, in Kofi Annan's 2004 Humanitarian Award speech, cited above, Dallaire becomes an embodiment and justification for the United Nations and Annan himself:

battered, humbled, but heroic and indispensable. By contrast, in right-wing US representations, like those pushed by the *Washington Times* shortly after President Bush's 2004 reelection, Dallaire is a text that proves the guilt of Annan and the uselessness of the United Nations: Dallaire warned Annan, but Annan did nothing. (American conservatives sponsored that story at that particular time, it may be remembered, as part of a coordinated attempt to oust Annan from office and weaken the UN—punishment for his failure to support Bush's invasion of Iraq.)[42]

But the most stunning renarration of Dallaire, and thus of the genocide itself, is going on right now at the ICTR. It is a renarration with what many believe are persuasive ethical claims of its own, based in the politics of left resistance to US neocolonialism. It is an attempt to undo Dallaire's work that is, like Dallaire's work, best seen as a contest over language—in fact, as a war over basic definitions.

Lawyer Peter Erlinder is angry at Dallaire. In March 2005, concluding a public talk he gave on the Rwandan genocide, Erlinder commented: "I saw the *New York Times* book section today and there's a big announcement that Dallaire's book is coming out in paperback, and I was so glad I was coming here to speak because I was really furious and at least I got some of that out." In the talk itself, he referred to Dallaire frequently with the acid of a defense lawyer, depicting him as obtuse, a dupe who fell for a setup of historic magnitude.

Erlinder, who served as the president of the National Lawyers Guild from 1993 to 1997, is an American professor of law who often litigates, pro bono, to defend political activists and to pursue claims of government and police misconduct. He is currently one of the counsel for the defense at the International Criminal Tribunal for Rwanda in the Bagosora trial, the highest priority of the military trials in Arusha, Tanzania (Colonel Théoneste Bagosora, a major power in the interim government, is alleged to have organized death squads and militias and to have armed the Interahamwe). When Dallaire appeared as a witness for the prosecution, Erlinder cross-examined him relentlessly. By the second day, Erlinder had successfully undermined Dallaire's confidence in his own memory of some of the most important facts of the genocide, including the famous "genocide fax" he had sent to Kofi Annan warning of a plan to exterminate Tutsis. It remains the most well-known evidence for the prosecution of a plan to commit genocide (Samantha Power calls it the "genocide's primary artifact");[43] yet Erlinder managed to get Dallaire to admit that he could not be sure where some of the most important information had come from, and that his informant, Jean-Pierre, had offered to move weapons to the MRND party building to help manufacture evidence of such a plot. To anybody familiar with the Rwandan genocide, this can only be described as an evidentiary bombshell.

Dallaire recalls coming to that cross-examination scared. "It was returning to hell again. After I went over the first time, in '98, I subsequently crashed and became a vegetable for nearly seven months. The second time, going for Bagosora, it wasn't elation and it wasn't revenge. It was doing the duty. However, there was grave concern that I wouldn't be able to testify properly, that the information would be garbled because of my pills and my state of mind, that I would not be able to be coherent. So my greatest fear was that my testimony would not support the prosecution's position."

Erlinder and Dallaire were in conflict even before Erlinder's cross-examination began. Erlinder so frequently objected to what he characterized as Dallaire's rambling narratives[44] that Dallaire interrupted the proceedings to seek assistance from the court: "Mr. President, if I may. I've been now at a state of starting to wonder if I'm being harassed by the Defence lawyer in regards to my responses to something he stated himself is so crucial as to my testimony on a genocide that happened not that

long ago."[45] When Erlinder insisted on yes-or-no answers,
Dallaire refused.

> E: *Frankly, General, with the long answers it's hard for me to figure*
> *out what it is that you mean.*
>
> D: *Well, I'm sorry to confuse you, and that is certainly not my ambi-*
> *tion, as what I have been trying to provide is more depth into the*
> *questions and the information surrounding the questions. We are*
> *not talking about a murder or traffic accident; we are talking about*
> *a country that went up in smoke. So it takes a little more than just*
> *staying to minute points without giving a context.*[46]

In the subsequent cross-examination of Brent Beardsley,
Dallaire's friend and closest colleague in Rwanda, the
witness put it more bluntly: "There are questions, sir, that
defy yes or no."[47] It was, so to speak, a conflict of episte-
mology. At one point Erlinder, in evident frustration,
called Dallaire "longwinded,"[48] and even went so far as to
interrupt a colleague's cross-examination with a passive-ag-
gressive request for assistance: he could not remember, he
claimed, what question had been asked by his colleague,
because the reply was so long (this earned a chastisement
from the court).[49] Their interaction was notably hostile,
even for a proceeding already markedly harsh. (One of the
primary strategies of the defense, for instance, was to dis-

credit Dallaire's testimony by questioning his competence; one attorney even asked if Dallaire might have been "intoxicated" or "brainwashed.")[50] Erlinder hounded him so aggressively and, at times, condescendingly, that Dallaire was driven to exasperation, insisting to the court that it was wrong for the defense to try to belittle him for coming from a "poor family"[51] (a heated misunderstanding) and finally exclaiming in frustration: "Oh, Jesus Christ."[52]

Dallaire later told me he thought Erlinder's conduct was unethical. "I find incredibly ironic," he said, "that it is an American trying to do that, with his country having been so beautifully absent in the whole exercise."

When I spoke with Erlinder, I wanted to find out above all what drove him. What made him so aggressive in defending the leaders of the Hutu military structure, when it seemed all the world believed they were responsible for the genocide? What made him so angry at people, like Dallaire, who were intent upon bringing to justice those whom the survivors identified as killers? Why was he defending these moral exiles?

"The real question," he told me, "is whether or not questions of fundamental fairness and due process are also part of the human rights regime." To have anything like a fair system, he continued, we cannot leave accusations untested. When I asked him if he worried that his work of testing accusations could hurt people, he said: "How do you test the recollection, the credibility of someone who all acknowledge has been horribly harmed and probably still suffers (if that is true)? All criminal defense lawyers have this difficult line to draw. . . . How is it that you can reveal the shortcomings in the testimony, or the ability to observe, or the recollection of the person who has been harmed without retraumatizing them—and sometimes that's not possible—or creating a situation where the sympathy for the person's pain ends up becoming more important than the quality of their evidence? It's hard to do that."

In the end, he said, "I have no moral ambivalence about what I'm doing." He believes the ICTR is something close to illegitimate, but he continues to fight there zealously, as any defense lawyer would, because he believes it is crucial to change the story we tell about Rwanda. It is a matter of duty. "The stories that have been told have been so one-sided and so condemnatory, almost in an unthinking way," he said. "My job as the defense lawyer in this proceeding is to make a record for history." Later he said two things that made it clear what this new story would mean to him. First: "International human rights norms are primarily applied against the less powerful by the more powerful." Second: "I view my job as interceding in unequal power relationships."

"There is no question that this is a one-sided undertaking," he said. This makes it difficult for him to do his work—he told me that his investigator has had to seek political asylum because of threats from the RPF-installed Rwandan government, and that the witnesses who come from Rwanda have been vetted in advance by the government and have to answer for their testimony when they come back. But despite this, because the court "has these juridical formations and juridical principles that can be used more or less skillfully, it's possible to create a factual record that proponents of a particular viewpoint might not have wished to be asked about." He continued: "What really is important here is that this record for history be made, so that to the extent that there was responsibility, that it be properly assigned and not be victor's justice."

What, then, is the story of Rwanda for Erlinder and the defense? I noticed that both in his public talk and in our conversation, Erlinder repeatedly referred to what happened in Rwanda as the "terrible tragedies." It struck me as an unusual phrasing for genocide, and he repeated it identically multiple times. Tragedies happen to people, they are not done to people, and in a sense that's what he believes about Rwanda. There was no plan for genocide, only a spontaneous, organic movement of violence, explicable by a long history of colonial manipulation and by more recent, war-bred paranoia on the part of the Hutus, who feared that exiled Tutsi aristocrats were coming back to Rwanda to subjugate them. In fact, if there's anybody to blame for the terrible tragedies, it must include the anglophone Rwandan Patriotic Front. As Erlinder puts it: "The invading [RPF] army understood that they could use that conflict [between Hutus and Tutsis], which was predictable after the beginning of the war . . . as an additional way to destabilize the country that they were invading. They also knew that if they didn't agree to the cease-fire and continued to press the war, that the Rwandan government would not have the military means, even theoretically, to be able to fight the war *and* stop the massacres." The massacres, in other words, were part of the "strategy of the invading army."[53] Erlinder cites hotly disputed accusations that the assassination of President Habyarimana (often described as the event that "triggered" the genocide) was coordinated by Paul Kagame, the RPF leader at the time and now the president of Rwanda. He notes, furthermore, that the United States had an interest in supporting the RPF against the francophone Hutu government as part of a plan to extend its influence in Africa. He points out that Kagame was trained in the United States.

There's another twist in the argument. In his 2005 talk, Erlinder spent a great deal of time explaining why Hutu and Tutsi were not ethnic identities. Here he points to the writings of leading academics like Mahmood Mamdani, who explain how the extreme Hutu/Tutsi division was generated through colonial management strategies—Hutu and Tutsi are, in other words, politically created identities. It wasn't at all clear why Erlinder spent so much time on this in his talk, so I followed up with him afterward. "A genocide has a particular definition," he explained. "A war is not a genocide. Killing civilians is not a genocide—it might be war crimes, but it's not a genocide. Genocide is people being killed because of their ethnic background and for nothing else. So if killing is taking place for political reasons, it's a politicide, not a genocide." In other words, there was no Rwandan genocide because there is no such thing as a Tutsi ethnicity that can be exterminated. "The question of who a Hutu is and who a Tutsi is," he said, "is completely without concrete meaning."

Eliahu Abram is an Israeli lawyer who has also worked on a trial for genocide, but on the opposing side. In the mid-1980s he was a member of the prosecuting team in Israel that indicted Ivan John Demjanjuk for participating in genocide at Treblinka (Abram is himself the child of a Holocaust survivor). When I asked Abram about the work, he recalled the emotional damage done to survivors under the brute skepticism of defense cross-examination. But, he added, the chasm separating experience from narration also made the work of prosecutors morally unsettling. He still worries over the indecencies involved in collecting testimony from survivors, in creating court-appropriate stories out of the unspeakable. "As a lawyer who is trying to translate this into evidence," he said, "you have to force yourself to deal with this like some kind of building block of some very matter-of-fact information. And this I think creates sometimes a kind of tension: 'What kind of human being am I if I'm dealing with this horrible information in such a practical, matter-of-fact way?' You have to distance yourself from the human aspect and deal with it as a technical matter in an extreme way."

In the time I spent with Erlinder, it seemed clear to me that he believed sincerely in what he was saying—this was not just a case of a lawyer playing a role—but also that his powerful conviction depended upon the thorough interior *technicalization* which playing a role required. For many, including me, hearing Erlinder challenge the memory of the genocide can be an upsetting experience. He is not surprised by this. But he is a forceful presence and he carries the heft of institutional authority. The one time I saw him give a public talk, in fact, the audience seemed eager to accept his arguments (perhaps because his account squares so easily with the views of groups predisposed to treat US

foreign policy with suspicion). Something he said at the
end of one of our conversations, however, made it seem to
me that his argument about the "fictional" genocide might
not work even by his own technical criteria. "Genocide,"
he explained at one point, "is based on the reasons the killing took place, the justifications or the psychological roots
of the exercise of improper power." It struck me when he
said this that if people *believed* they were eliminating an
ethnic group, if the killers' justifications and psychological
motivations were about ethnicity, then it might not matter
whether or not the ethnicity in question was, so to speak, a
fiction. It's genocide because they thought it was genocide
when they were doing it, because that is the story they told
themselves.[54]

The Rwandan genocide was, from the start, a conflict over terminology. Most of the attempts at renaming
were obvious and grotesque. The killing itself was called
"work"; kidnapping and raping a woman was called taking
a "wife"; innocent civilians trying to cross roadblocks were
labeled "infiltrators."[55] Even the UN participated in this re-
sponsibility-erasing language. The code cable announcing
that the UN was planning to withdraw its forces as the killings accelerated included a request to Dallaire for an as-

sessment of what would happen to those who had "taken refuge" at UN sites (they were massacred). Dallaire comments: "I noted the use of the phrase 'taken refuge' as opposed to 'under UN protection.'"[56]

In the immediate aftermath of the genocide, the Western media used language that went even further, insulating everyone from responsibility for everything. Televised images of Hutus—not Tutsis—dying of cholera in refugee camps confirmed the media theme: senseless chaos. Philip Gourevitch was one of the first journalists to report in detail about the genocide, precisely because this rhetoric convinced him we didn't know the real story. As he put it to me: "The language that's used most frequently in the popular response to something like Rwanda are words like 'unspeakable,' 'unthinkable,' 'unimaginable.' And [in the case of Rwanda] those all struck me as words that ultimately were telling you not to speak, think, or understand, that they basically are words that get you off the hook and then in a sense give you license for both kinds of ignorance: literal ignorance—not knowing—and ignoring."

By most accounts, Gourevitch's reporting and his book, *We Wish to Inform You That Tomorrow We Will Be Killed with Our Families,* changed how the Western media reported the story. The book has been assigned reading in high schools across the country and in several hundred courses at hundreds of US colleges and universities, from the Air Force Academy to Yale University (one prosecutor at the ICTR asserted that many at the court read it as an introduction to understanding the genocide).

I would like to close this chapter by juxtaposing Gourevitch's sense of the difference this makes with the perspectives of two young UN employees I spoke with immediately after my conversation with him. The contrast seems to me to exemplify the wide range of our attitudes toward the power of stories. Gourevitch said rather candidly that he is not at all sanguine about the positive effects of his work—indeed, about the real world effects of any storytelling. He recalled doing a story about the opening of the Holocaust Museum in Washington, D.C.: "People were congratulating themselves on taking the right stand against the Holocaust in 1993, and telling us how this museum was a monument to the fact that we would never let such a thing happen again. And that was when Srebrenica was falling for the first time. And then a year later, when I went back to the museum for a follow-up piece, it was when Rwanda was happening." He paused. "Now it's Darfur."

He continued with a story about the uselessness of stories; in its paradoxically unforgettable depiction of forgettability, it reminded me of Diop's account of the scavenging dogs in Rwanda.[57] Gourevitch once published an article for the *New Yorker* that received a lot of attention, he recalled. It was about a man named Girumuhatse who was living undisturbed in his home village in Rwanda. Through painstaking fact-checking and persistence, Gourevitch proved that Girumuhatse had run a roadblock during the genocide and was responsible for the murder of perhaps as many as seventy of his neighbors. Gourevitch distributed copies of the story to officials at the Ministry of Justice in Kigali. Two months later he returned to do another story. When he met the government officials, they brought up the story and said how terrible it was that such a man had returned to his village with impunity. They then asked Gourevitch curiously, "Whatever happened to that guy?"

"But I'm not of the school of thought that says it's all futile," he qualified. "Sometimes the stories we tell about these things do change things; they make a difference. But is it a good difference? I don't know. If I tell a story and you're moved by it, I can't account for how you'll be moved by it or what you'll do with it. Ignoring it made me uncomfortable, so I wrote about it. But I didn't have any illusions about making things better." He tried to explain what he meant with what amounted to a parable about the good of humanitarian work:

I was in Sri Lanka right after the tsunami [in December 2004] and I was talking to a de-miner there. Now de-mining, that's the supercool of all humanitarian activities, because (a) it's a pretty unambiguous good; (b) it's kind of hairy and a little insane; and (c) it actually requires a certain level of expertise and know-how. They're like firemen. You know, you go to these far-out places and you remove these things and then you blow them up, which is cool, if you're into that kind of thing. But mostly it really is pretty morally unambivalent. Great, you're removing explosives that are buried in the ground in areas that are no longer immersed in conflict, and a lot of people are able to move back to these areas. And they come back and they can let their little children run around without losing their legs, their cattle don't blow up, and it's better, right? Great. It's a net wash good.

So I'm talking to this one de-miner, but we're talking about the larger political situation, which is: there's a cease-fire and there's a suspension of hostilities, but basically the place is still totally at war and there's a reasonably high probability that at some point it will get really nasty again. And she said, at one stage, "You know, I can't help wondering if what

we're doing is actually bad, because we're making areas safe in order to lure people to come back to them
from where they've gone in displacement. What
we're basically doing is repopulating the front line
just in time for it to get bad. If it blows up again, it's
arguable that what we did was worse than nothing."

The unpredictability of consequences is equally dramatic
in the case of morally persuasive representations. As the
case of *I, Rigoberta Menchú* reveals, the well-told story of
suffering can generate as much suspicion and alienation as
sympathy and action. When first published, the book drew
worldwide attention to the plight of the oppressed Quiché
Indians in Guatemala and earned the Nobel Peace Prize
for Menchú—but in the late 1990s it became a scandal that
occasioned public discrediting of "'human rights' leftists"
when anthropologist David Stoll charged Menchú with
fabricating key details of her story.[58] Kay Schaffer and
Sidonie Smith take this as an emblem of the radical contin-
gency of reception:

Those who publish their stories of oppression, abuse,
trauma, degradation, and loss can neither know nor
control how that story will be received and interpreted. A story can generate recognition, empathy,

critical awareness, advocacy, and activism elsewhere that helps to empower people struggling locally to extend their campaigns for human rights. The same story can become a commodity, and the teller a celebrity on a world stage, as the narrative is dispersed through book clubs, radio and television interviews, and talk shows, classrooms, and living rooms, picked up by independent documentary filmmakers, and distributed internationally.

But as *I, Rigoberta Menchú* reveals, "the same story can become a 'scandal' overseas that produces resistance within and beyond the boundaries of the nation." It can, Schaffer and Smith conclude, "produce a backlash of actions that forestall recognition and redress."[59]

Representations can misfire because of imperturbable bystander passivity and because of malicious intervention by perpetrators and enablers through media counter-representations. They can fail because they are too familiar, because their discouraging repetition makes us believe help might be applied more effectively elsewhere;[60] and they can fail because they are too unfamiliar, because their content has not yet reached the necessary "discursive threshold"[61] required to make it through the filters of information-overloaded news consumers. They can be re-

jected in the global North because accepting their reality
can require first acknowledging our complicity, guilt, or
the ways we benefit from systemic violations; and they can
be rejected in the global South because they are experienced as hypocritical imperialist incursions on state sover-
eignty ("We are jealous defenders of [a country's] right to
self-determination," an air force spokesman declared on
behalf of the Argentinean junta during the infamous Dirty
War in the late 1970s and early 1980s. "That is why we
will not allow [groups] waving banners for 'human rights'
to determine . . . our future").[62] They can fail because
they are too vivid, causing us to look away, and because
they are not vivid enough, leaving us complacent.[63] They
can fail because they are too statistical, giving us none of
the personal drama that moves us, and because they are
too personal, giving us no sense of urgent magnitude.[64]
Even when they succeed they can be failures: as Fiona
Terry observes, aid organizations "must amplify the grav-
ity of a situation or selectively report the worst aspects of
it in order to arouse sufficient awareness and action to
raise a response," thereby generating short-term funding
at the risk of long-term desensitization.[65] "The flood of
information in the world today," William Shawcross remarks, "sometimes seems not to further but to retard education; not to excite but to dampen curiosity; not to en-

lighten, but to dismay. The poet Archibald MacLeish once noted, 'We are deluged with facts but we have lost or are losing our human ability to feel them.'"[66]

On the airplane to New York to meet with Gourevitch, I read a book by a young forensic anthropologist named Clea Koff. *The Bone Woman,* translated into nine languages and published in fourteen countries, tells the story of Koff's work for the UN collecting evidence from mass graves for the International Criminal Tribunal for Rwanda.[67] Her sunny optimism in the grimmest of places, and her faith in the positive consequences of her storytelling, provided an almost startling contrast to Gourevitch's abiding sense of the tragedy of good intentions. Her inspiration as a college student, she wrote, was, in fact, a book: Christopher Joyce and Eric Stover's *Witnesses from the Grave: The Stories Bones Tell.* "I had known for years that my goal was to help end human rights abuses by proving to would-be killers that bones can talk."[68] In Koff's account of the work, she describes "listening" to the bones, interpreting "the skeleton's language," telling its "story."[69] In Rwanda she saw herself quite explicitly as a storyteller, and as one whose stories could not help but make a difference.

> If someone had asked me about my career goal on
> my first mission to Rwanda, I would have said that I

aspired to give voice to people silenced by their own governments or militaries, people suppressed in the most final way: murdered and put into clandestine graves. Looked at from this perspective, working for the two United Nations international criminal tribunals as a forensic expert really was a dream come true for me. I felt this most keenly my first day on the job in Rwanda: I was crouched on a forty-five-degree slope, under a heavy canopy of banana leaves and ripe avocados, placing red flags in the dark soil wherever I found human remains. Let's put it this way: I ran out of flags. I went back to my room that night and wrote in my journal about the realization of a dream. And I kept on writing.[70]

Koff's commitment to the work in Rwanda was professional but also personal: a woman of African descent, she has family in three of the surrounding countries. When one reporter asked Koff how she dealt with death and the families of the dead, what she thought while digging down through the soil to the men, women, and children below, she answered gently, "I'm thinking: 'We're coming. We're coming to take you out.'"[71] Over the years, she told me, many of her colleagues became demoralized by the work, pulling people out of mass graves in one country only to hear of fresh ones being created elsewhere. Koff never did. She was well known in the field as the young woman who, crouched among rotting corpses, always smiled.

(Koff's right to tell the story of the dead she recovered, by the way, has never been questioned, but the fact that *she* told the story sometimes has been. On her book tours, she told me, she has encountered people who assumed somebody else wrote the book for her.)

Against the good of the ICTR, where Koff's stories found their final official purpose, Gourevitch argues that because officials decided to locate the ICTR in Arusha, Tanzania, rather than in Rwanda, millions of dollars in funding that could have gone toward building up Rwanda's own capacity for justice were diverted to a temporary structure that symbolized, for Rwandans, the world's doubt in their capacity for self-governance. Diop concurs, citing the Tribunal as one more instance when the images and stories defining Africans are controlled by non-Africans. "Arusha is too far away from where the genocide took place, and the victims are unaware of what is going on. . . . Most of the Rwandans I met do not believe that the Tribunal is to be taken seriously." In the end, he charges, "the trials are useless and simply reflect the hypocrisy of the international community."

Others have criticized both the Rwandan and the Yugo-

slavian criminal tribunals—along with the concept of tribunals altogether, arguing that they justify themselves at
least in part on the demonstrably false assumption of their
"deterrence" value. Armed fighters who grant humanitarian workers safe access to victims in conflict zones will, it
is reported, sometimes ask to be remembered for their
humane conduct if they are ever brought to court—but
that's cold comfort to critics. As skeptics have said to Koff,
the fear of accountability did not make Serbian troops
and police in Kosovo reluctant to kill civilians—the fear of
accountability made them remove the bodies from the
mass graves, hide them, or burn them. Koff replies to this
range of criticisms with a harder-edged, narrower optimism. "There are those that criticize the Tribunal for being
too slow and for holding the trials outside the affected re-
gion," she told me. "But it is actually holding people ac-
countable, and marking individual rather than collective
responsibility for these crimes. It's something we haven't
had since Nuremberg, and we need to support that." And
when people feel pressured to hide bodies, she added, this
creates "a larger physical trail of behavior that shows the
perpetrators knew that what they were doing was illegal."
This deprives them of the standard denial stories employed
in post-genocidal societies: it was a war; confusion was
rife; there was no plan. This alone, she believes, is a kind
of progress. Koff has been dogged by nightmares, and has

found herself in the grip of vivid, resurgent emotions that cause her to weep in the worst of places—while driving on the highway, while giving public talks about her book. But she has never doubted.

On that same trip to New York I also met Aida Mengistu, a young Ethiopian woman who had joined the UN's Office for the Coordination of Humanitarian Affairs (OCHA) with the "dream" of returning to Africa and being able "to do something." She had just returned from Darfur, where the genocide was continuing into its third year. She had been working there since the early stages of the massacres. At the time, it was believed that at least 300,000 people had been killed and approximately 2.5 million had fled their homes. Human Rights Watch reported indiscriminate killing of civilians, mass gang-rapes, sexual mutilation, abduction of infants, and a systematic practice of destroying wells and granaries to make survival at assaulted sites impossible (the World Health Organization projected that 10,000 displaced people would die each month from illness and malnutrition when the rains began).[72] It was, for many, the final death of the idea of "Never Againism," as Gourevitch put it. That very week, as the UN was working to coordinate humanitarian assistance for Darfur's displaced civilians, the United States Congress proposed cutting its UN dues payments.

When Mengistu and I spoke, she had been home a mat-

ter of days. She told me she was excited about her new job
in the Advocacy and Public Information Section. You can
change things with this sort of work, she insisted, even in
places like Darfur. The international community had, after
all, intervened this time in a way it hadn't with Rwanda,
and it did so precisely because of the work of humanitarian storytelling—in the United States, most prominently,
because of Emily Wax's reporting in the *Washington Post*
and Nicholas Kristof's columns and photographs in the
New York Times. (When the Darfur Accountability Act was
introduced in the US Senate, articles by Kristof were cited
and photos he had chosen were displayed; the Sudanese
government blamed him for the sanctions imposed on Sudan.)[73] The success of these representations in turn, according to journalists like Stephen Smith, depended largely
upon the collective retroactive narrations of Rwanda (and
the fact that the tenth-anniversary memorials of its genocide occurred in 2004), which put the Bush administration
in the position of having to acknowledge the genocide in
Darfur and, once committing to that, having to at least appear to be doing something.

For many, however, *appearance* was the key issue. The
intervention was narrow: humanitarian assistance was provided and, in Kristof's carefully chosen words, pressure
was applied that caused "a reduced rate of slaughter by the

Sudanese government."[74] As Nathalie Civet, head of the Médecins Sans Frontières mission in Sudan, put it in comments before the United Nations Security Council shortly after I met Mengistu: "How can I convey how a woman living in a camp feels when she goes out each day to fetch firewood knowing that she may be attacked, robbed, beaten, or even raped? How can I tell you what it is like for her to then rush back not to miss the general food distribution, if it is even happening, then cook the food while also not forgetting to bring her sick child to the feeding centre?" Civet concluded that Darfur's displaced millions were in "humanitarian limbo": "Despite all its improvements, aid is still inadequate and precarious even in areas that are relatively easily accessible by aid agencies, such as the big camps and settlements of displaced people in or near the regional capitals. . . . Two years after having fled their homes because of violence and fear, they remain living in humiliating conditions with no end in sight."[75] What will happen in Darfur as stories like Civet's begin to circulate? Caroline Moorehead speculates that the interest the US government has in promoting action in Darfur has decreased as the interest US companies have in developing Sudan's oil wealth has increased, and that Washington's growing partnership with Khartoum over intelligence in the "war on terror" has contributed to a high-level policy

of ignoring the stories humanitarian workers are trying
to tell.[76]

Mengistu knew these things as well as anyone; but
whenever she acknowledged them to me, she did so in a
tone that I can only describe as a tone of *preparation*—as if
she were thinking about what she could say next, as if she
were thinking, "Yes, that's true, that's true, but let me try
to show you what we can do." What Mengistu believed
could be accomplished by telling the story of Darfur might
have had something to do with the idealism of the young,
or, alternatively, with a chastened realism, a willingness to
accept *less-thans*. It may have been the consequence-blind
feeling of purpose that comes from simply trying, the faith
we cling to because it is the basis of our will to act, or the
confidence that comes from immersion in an institutional
culture that performs effectiveness in its very architecture
(the disproportion that is characteristic of the UN's headquarters in New York—the imbalance between the high-
rise glass slab of the Secretariat Building and its immediate
surround—is the disproportion of authority itself).

Whatever it was, it was strong and sincere, even after
two years of watching the world watch another Rwanda.
"I think people just need to be aware of what's going on,"
Mengistu told me. "Maybe they don't know. I do think that

people are good and ethical and would like to help if they knew that these kinds of things happen." She had been nervous when we began our interview but at this point was positively beaming. "If people were aware enough, they could make a difference."

2 INTERROGATION

To enter the headquarters of the United Nations High Commissioner for Refugees in Ankara, Turkey, you must pass through barbed-wire gates and a security checkpoint. If you are seeking UN protection as a refugee (because you have escaped Iraq after being raped and tortured or because you will be executed if forced to return to Iran), you will be escorted through these gates and then taken downstairs to the holding chambers in the basement. There you will be required to answer a series of questions to determine whether or not you meet the specific conditions for refugee status under international law. If your answers do not suffice, you will be deported back to your country of origin. The interview rooms are small and poorly ventilated. Larry Bottinick, eligibility officer for the UNHCR, explained when we met there that they would be moving to a new building soon. "Whenever you ask an Iraqi to de-

scribe the conditions of their detention," he said of refugees from Saddam Hussein's Iraq, "they answer: 'It was
like this room.'"

But this chapter is not about what it feels like to be
interrogated. It is about what it feels like to interrogate
someone. Through a series of formal and informal interviews, I document here the organizational dynamics and
communicative practices of some of the world's most recognizable "humanitarian inquisitors": the UNHCR, the International Committee of the Red Cross (ICRC), and the
Human Rights Association (HRA). I examine how their
different organizational goals shape their language practices and how these, in turn, either amplify or diminish their
capacity for dealing with state-sponsored violence. I focus in
particular on the everyday practices of activists in the field,
hoping to better understand not only how we can use language to alter the operations of violence but also to see
how, by using language in such ways, we might be altered.

Each of these three organizations seeks to eliminate
physical suffering by using words. They do certain types of
language work (personal interviews, investigation of document trails) that enable them to perform certain types of
speech acts (the UNHCR announces, "This person is a refugee"; the ICRC declares, "You are guilty of violating international norms"). The daily work of rescue is a matter

of words instead of deeds—or, rather, of words *as* deeds. One ICRC delegate explained: "For outsiders, and to get money from sponsor governments, what you have to show is airplanes, and big trucks full of food, and field hospitals filled and packed with wounded people—because this type of work can be shown. But most of the work that we do is just talking. Really, what is at the heart of the ICRC is to make representations."

The fundamental representational task of the ICRC, like that of the UNHCR and the HRA, is to document harm. The work ranges from compiling comprehensive reference indices culled from secondhand data to making firsthand visual confirmations. One UNHCR legal officer described an interview she'd conducted with a woman whose face had been so severely burned during her torture that the only recognizably human features that remained were the holes where her eyes and lips should have been. The officer found it hard to know if and where she should look. Another worker from a different organization gave me a list he'd created of the torture techniques his nation currently uses, with frequency variations. It reads as follows.

psychological coercion and physical deprivation while in
    detention:
        insults, isolation, blindfolding, mock executions; forcing
    prisoners to declare obedience to the state, to kiss boots, to

shout slogans, to obey nonsensical orders, to listen to the
screams of tortured persons; depriving prisoners of food,
water, sleep, needed medicines, heat, bedding; forbidding
urination or defecation, or confining prisoners in holes full
of human urine and feces
physical assault:
    beating and punching the head, the hands, the soles of
the feet; beating with hoses or other implements, wrapping
in wet blankets and beating; spraying with cold or pressur-
ized water, forcing the head under water, pulling out hair,
pushing down stairs or dropping from heights, suspending
upside-down from parallel hangers; electrocution, freezing,
burning, strangling
sexual abuse and assault:
    forcing prisoners to strip naked, to have intercourse with
spouses in the presence of security officers, to perform sexually taboo practices, including intercourse with friends of
the same sex or with one's own children; beating the genitals, squeezing and twisting testicles and nipples; rape by
single or multiple assailants, rape with blunt or sharp objects.

This chapter is about what it is like to be the person
who maintains such a list, the person whose job it is to
document pain, to bring it into language—not as a special
crisis mission in dissolving states, like the mission of
Roméo Dallaire, but as a daily bureaucratic routine in es-

tablished institutional structures. One of the most striking
things about such work is that, in the organizations that
use language as rescue, some of the most damaging stress
results not from witnessing suffering but from the nature
of the organization's rules and goals for communication.
What uses are these surrogate voices designed to serve?
How do inquisitorial organizations train their officers to
structure dialogue, to document, to report? How are the
words of the survivor translated into the officially sanctioned vocabulary of the institution? In other words, what,
for the organization, counts as language in the first place?
The various tactics of these three organizations—the
UNHCR, the ICRC, and the HRA—illustrate the full spectrum of the representational strategies available to human
rights activists and humanitarian workers, from using language as a precise tool for objective, agent-neutral mea-
surement to using it as a form of emotional exhortation
and moral coercion. As we shall see, the moral risks and
strategic compromises these organizations make in finding
their place along that spectrum are embodied most dramatically in the psychic double-binds that structure the
daily lives of their workers.

The UNHCR, as a global organization, provides
temporary relief for thousands of refugees each year, in

countries ranging from Bosnia to Rwanda, and resettles
a smaller number permanently in host countries like Swe-
den and the United States. At the UNHCR in Turkey, legal officers are responsible for determining the status of
men, women, and children who have fled from one of the
world's most troubled regions: Iraq, Iran, and Afghanistan.
The work they do is difficult; the hours are long, the stakes
are high, and the mission is excruciatingly specific. The job
of people like Larry Bottinick, who gave up a lucrative position as a corporate lawyer because he wanted to do good
in the world, is to weed people *out*. He explains: "You have
people who need protection but cannot receive it, according to refugee law as we must apply it in Turkey. We have
to be fairly strict: we are the guardians of a specific convention. There are people who tear at your heart but whom
you just cannot help. You get people who are in miserable,
miserable conditions, but who are not refugees. Those are
the hardest cases." And then there are those you are required to help. The combination can be difficult to accept.
One legal officer recalled being forced to deny protection
to victims of brutal rape and unceasing domestic violence,
even as she was granting refugee status to a brothel owner.

The criteria for determining who is a refugee are laid
out in the 1951 United Nations Refugee Convention and
in the extensive case law that has developed around it. The
definition is relatively simple. A refugee is a person who

has a "well-founded fear of being persecuted for reasons of race, religion, nationality, membership of a particular social group or political opinion."[1] But interpreting the definition is difficult; the phrase "well-founded fear" alone has generated countless pages of legal commentary. While officers study the details of cases and struggle with problems of legal interpretation (is there a "reasonable chance" of persecution? what constitutes "persecution"? how do you define a "particular" social group?), applicants wait. Cases can take several months to decide. Seda Kuzucu, a young Turkish woman with seven years' experience as a legal officer (a lifetime in this position, given the burnout rate), explains the problems this can cause: "When decision periods increase, violence at home increases also. They cannot work, so they are working illegally. Children cannot go to school. We are trying our best to enroll them. Women cannot work because of the home culture, sometimes; or they become forced prostitutes. We have limitations on the assistance we are able to give."

Legal officers like Seda and Larry are the gatekeepers to the freedom of refugee resettlement. Manipulation and misinformation are, therefore, the background of their job. There is, indeed, a market of goods and services aimed at helping claimants deceive legal officers. Larry recalled one case in particular. "During a break in the interview, the interpreter asked if he could borrow the asylum seeker's newspaper. The person said yes, but in the folds of the newspaper was a sheet with the questions we would ask and the answers they should give. It said for one: 'You should hesitate and tell them you don't want to say because you are afraid your family will be hurt back in your country of origin. They will promise confidentiality, and then you tell them the following.'" Larry smiled. "And the man had been doing exactly what it said."

Even those who truly merit refugee status will lie if they believe another story will be more likely to succeed, if they believe they will harm somebody else by telling the truth, or if they wish to hide how they managed to enter the country. "Human nature being what it is, when someone lies to us we think they're a liar," Larry comments. "You have to put that aside. Someone can lie and still be a refugee." Legal officers, Larry explains, have several strategies for cross-checking facts and gauging the consistency of stories during interviews, and he emphasized that they work carefully to determine which lies are irrelevant and which are material to the final decision. It is slow work.

But sometimes the problem in getting the information needed for a decision is not lying. Sometimes it is silence. People fail to tell their stories for many reasons: shame, confusion, the willed forgetting that comes with trauma.

One man was nearly denied refugee status because an un-
detected hearing problem brought about by torture and
head injuries interfered with his ability to respond to questions. Another was almost turned away because his response was distorted. The dates and facts of his story did
not match up, and officers assumed he was lying—until a
translator's mistake was discovered and corrected. Many
torture survivors become resistant and hostile when interviewed. Eye contact that lasts a fraction of a second
too long, a sudden shift in bodily posture, the sound of a
door opening unexpectedly—any number of small cues
can trigger fear reactions and defensive silence. Whatever
the cause, the consequences are extreme: if applicants do
not tell their stories as they must, they will be deported.
You must get them talking. "If they are not cooperative in
the interview," says Seda, describing a last-resort pressure
tactic for getting people to talk, "I can tell them I have the
right to end the interview."

The interview is structured like a triangle, comprising
legal officer, applicant, and translator. The legal officer asks
a question; the translator translates it to the applicant; the
applicant replies to the translator while the legal officer
enters notes into a computer; and then the translator turns
to the legal officer and translates. The system is not designed to foster intimacy. Emotion can be dangerous. As

one translator explained: "It is hard. You should not show any sympathy to the ICs [individual claimants]. They will say what they think is affecting you and you will not get to the facts. They will try to make pressure on you. They will try to manipulate you; they will hold you responsible. People cry and you must sit there." When I asked this translator how she handled it, she told me that for now she is able to bear it. She works with a legal officer who is very sensitive—when she needs to stop the interview so that she can cry in private, the legal officer can tell just by looking at her. "I had nightmares in the beginning, really nightmares. My hands shake like that," the translator said, holding out her hands and laughing. "With time, this is better. But my son still complains. He says how now all the time I am sleeping."

The interviews give victims a chance to tell their story, but they are not therapy sessions. The primary job of the legal officers is to obtain the information necessary for an accurate evaluation. And they must be strict. Countries offering residency and protection to refugees will continue to do so only if they have faith that the UNHCR is applying the law objectively, as it has been agreed upon internationally, instead of using the law to help people for whom they have sympathy. "This is a norm we must defend," says Meltem Çiçekli, a legal officer with a mournful alto voice

who was once a refugee herself. "It is a right, and we must
not confuse the concept."

Not confusing the concept means deporting many. But
for the legal officers there are serious consequences to
weeding people out. People who have fled their home
countries live without assistance in Turkey while their cases
are considered; after a decision has been announced, they
remain for some time before they can be deported. This
means they can *react*. One man who was denied refugee
status protested the decision by sewing his mouth shut
with a crude needle and thread. Another waited for his
legal officer to appear outside the building and then threw
his own infant child under the wheels of a speeding taxi-
cab. "This is your fault!" he cried. Larry has been followed to his car at night. Seda cannot post her name on
the doorbell panel at her apartment complex. Threats are
frequently made against the office. Walking through the
building, I saw many security alerts posted on the walls—
photographs of men with descriptions beneath and warn-
ings to contact Security.

But this also is background. "They are sometimes
threatening our lives," Seda says flatly. "But I am used to
this." When asked to recall their most difficult experiences,
the legal officers did not talk about danger or fear of repri-
sal; they talked about the daily challenge of remaining objective. When pressed, they each had one particular experi-

ence that they were still struggling with. Seda's story was typical, insofar as any of the stories could be typical. The case involved sexual torture.

> It was three years ago. She is a young woman. She did not want me to write anything. I take my hands from the computer and even my interpreter is not writing anything. And she told everything, every detail—I can't stop her—she is screaming, shouting, crying, laughing. I can't do anything, I was just watching her. And she told all the story, and it was really bad. It was on Friday, I remember. The next day all of my body is full of bumps, these red bumps.
>
> She attempted to suicide two times while I have to decide the case. I put the case aside; I can't decide. I can't. I am so much emotionally attached to this woman. I gave it to one of the senior officers: finally we reject the case, but on reopening it was accepted.
>
> She's accepted, so I'm happy. Maybe it is not with me, but I'm happy one of our officers saw it. But I can't do it. I know if I will accept, it is because I am emotionally attached. It was my first case of divorce and domestic violence.

In Geneva later that month, I spoke to Barthold Bierens de Haan, psychiatrist for the ICRC, about the psychological pressures of humanitarian work. He described it through the metaphor of disease. "The suffering of the victims brings secondary traumatization to the witness," he explained. "Trauma is an infection which is going from one person to the other." But to understand the depression that commonly afflicts humanitarian workers, he continued, it is perhaps best not to think of individual traumatic exposures; to focus solely on the single terrible story is to misunderstand the chronic psychic friction of the work. The most damaging stress is often cumulative. The psychological problems hardest to address, he explained, are matters of repetitive strain.

Work at the UNHCR is repetitive strain. "At some point as an interviewer, you get very cynical," says Larry. "You hear the same stories again and again." To address this problem, the UNHCR allows international staffers to rotate positions. After a difficult post in Indonesia, Larry was moved to Guantánamo Bay and then to Prague. In some cases, such rotations change nothing but geography. But even though a new posting may involve essentially the same job, it is still an important fresh start: the regional information is new, the populations are new, and the stories are new. Just as significant, rotation can offer periods of respite amid first-world living conditions. "Microwave, CNN, ocean" was Larry's summary of Guantánamo Bay.

"It's essential to rotate positions, particularly between easy and difficult posts," Larry asserted. "Sometimes people should be *forced* to do this. I can think of one person who went from difficult assignment to difficult assignment to difficult assignment, and ended up killing himself." Yet avoiding burnout through periodic rotation to less stressful sites also means that workers must continually adapt to unfamiliar environments; just when a home is becoming comfortable and familiar, it is time to leave. Bierens de Haan calls this sort of environmental alienation "basic stress," and emphasizes that its effects can be serious and long term. The disorientation can be severe to the point of comedy. Larry lived in a tin shack while conducting Vietnamese status-determination interviews, and one morning a rooster entered his hovel and began to crow. The noise reverberated wildly, and Larry thought to himself yearningly: "This would never happen if I were back in D.C.—that rooster would *never* get by my secretary."

Some workers for the UNHCR, however, cannot even rotate. The organization relies upon two pools of employees in any field office: international careerists, often from industrialized nations in Europe and North America, who occupy leadership roles (people like Larry, who is an eligibility officer); and the locals, typically functioning as subordinate legal officers and translators. In Ankara, the Turks lucky enough to find such work seldom rise high enough in the organization to rotate out to other countries, and often cannot possibly think of giving up their job despite cumulative stress, because these positions offer stable, well-paying work in a nation where neither is widely available.

At dinner late one night with several legal officers, mostly Turks, I asked what they did to get by. They laughed and said there was always alcohol, cigarettes, and sex. (It has been said of humanitarian work that sometimes it entails more passion than protection.) But the officers also talked about the respectful friendships that developed in field offices. Marco, a young Italian junior professional, worked in a remote rural field post with Meltem Çiçekli. They had nothing in their village but their work and each other's company. Each night they would meet together and discuss cases and legal theory, Meltem cynically but compassionately mocking Marco's idealism. They would argue and drink and smoke and laugh and cry. "You're responsible for the health of your colleagues, as well as your own," Larry had said earlier that day, in response to a question about periods of extreme work stress. "You make sure you all have regular meals. You have a buddy system." The camaraderie of Marco and Meltem clearly helped them to bear their stress and isolation, but it also seemed to me that it created a closed network: there was no aspect of their life that was not refugee work. They had nowhere to go that was *outside*. Their solution to stress, like the solution of the rotation system itself, created its own unique degenerative cycles, and this mirrored the double-bind of the organization as a whole: to protect the vulnerable from injury, you must treat them as opponents; but in treating them as opponents, you subject them to injury. So I asked again: What helped the officers to continue? What was their way out?

Seda pointed with her thumb at Meltem, who had recently taken a break from work. "She has had a tough month," Seda said. Meltem's last two cases had ended badly. She'd had to reject both. One had then mutilated himself and the other had attempted suicide.

"Meltem had a nervous breakdown," Seda said, touching Meltem's shoulder and looking in her eyes as she spoke about her in the third person.

Meltem nodded her head and smiled.

"Finally," she said.

■■■■■ Pascal Daudin spent many years interviewing detainees for the ICRC. He discusses the work now in a muted, weary voice and efficient, almost businesslike manner that masks what one colleague described in an aside as a "heart of gold." I visited him at the ICRC's quiet hilltop headquarters in bustling Geneva. To reach his office, located near the ICRC Museum, I had to pass between the rental cars of placid vacationers looking for famous European tourist spots and the trucks displaying the Red Cross and Red Crescent that, in my mind, were inseparable from images of starvation and warfare. The strange coupling of opposites in the headquarters' physical landscape seemed an appropriate symbol for the paradoxes of all the ICRC's humanitarian work: resist war by accepting it; overcome tyrants by cooperating with them. Pascal's work with nonmilitary detainees was no exception. Like Larry and Seda, he described the process of interviewing victims of abuse as a terrible balancing act. To protect those who have been tortured and interrogated, you must interrogate them. "You have to get general information on the places of detention," Pascal said firmly. "You have to interrogate people— as softly as possible—but you have to interrogate people."

The ICRC has an international mandate to operate in a variety of ways in humanitarian crises all over the world. The ICRC is everywhere. Other relief organizations fled Rwanda during the genocide, but the ICRC remained.[2] When expatriate ICRC staff were evacuated from Afghanistan in 2001, the world held its breath. The stage was set for catastrophe and now *nobody* would be there to help.

Whatever dramatic international crisis happens to be at the center of Western media attention, the ICRC is often the first and last (and sometimes only) humanitarian group there. But one of the ICRC's most important and enduring missions is also the one that receives the least media attention (unless it happens at a US military base): the daily work of visiting civilians detained on security grounds in crisis zones across the globe.

ICRC visits to prisons have several basic purposes. ICRC delegates keep records of detainees to prevent disappearances and to restore contact with families; in extreme cases, they provide material relief such as medicine or food; and most important, they interview prisoners to obtain information about conditions of detention. Evidence of neglect or abuse is then collected in reports that are passed on to higher authorities within the government, along with demands for redress. This is the final objective.

The ICRC's ability to get access to prisons in nations where torture is policy and disappearances the goal depends upon a series of chastening compromises and a complicated balance of interests. Governments acquire some degree of international legitimacy by being able to say they have allowed ICRC delegates into the country. And the ICRC makes two basic and reassuring promises. First, they will not operate as moral judges or as the partisans of prisoners. They will remain neutral and listen to arguments from both sides, recognizing that prisoners, like guards, are capable of lying to promote their interests. ICRC delegates, in short, are advocates for humane standards, not for particular humans. "'Judgment' is not a term very much used in the ICRC," Pascal explains. "The key word is 'dialogue,' not 'judgment.'" The second promise the ICRC gives has been described as a deal with the devil (in fact, the foundational myth of Médecins Sans Frontières is that it was originated by ICRC workers who renounced the organization because they believed this promise had made them complicit in genocide). They promise they will not reveal information about what they discover to anyone outside the government they are investigating. Evidence of atrocities is provided only to the government whose security forces are perpetrating the atrocities, and to no one else.[3]

Listening to Pascal's first descriptions, I expressed skepticism about the ICRC's ability to achieve anything of real value under such conditions. But Pascal had no doubts. "I am not a prison tourist," he said. The work, he explained, is very upsetting and traumatic, and if he did not believe it could make an important difference he would not undertake it. Pascal's colleague Jean-Jacques Frésard described how the ICRC had brought about dramatic changes in the treatment of prisoners throughout Iraq over a period of several years. Nelson Mandela, recalling ICRC visits during apartheid, claimed that "improvements in the conditions of our imprisonment at Robben Island were to a large measure due to the pressure that the mere presence of the Red Cross brought to bear on our jailer-regime."[4] Indeed, as he is reported to have said at the time, such ICRC work should be measured not only by the goods it brings but also by the harms it prevents—counterfactuals as unmeasurable as they are terrifying. But in reports compiled by Pascal, Hernán Reyes, and Marina Staiff, the list of accomplishments seemed much more humble. Negotiating to allow prisoners to keep small personal possessions. Submitting requests for longer visits from families. Alleviating a male prisoner's concerns that his beatings have rendered him permanently impotent. Making sure Muslim detainees have frequent access to water for ritual ablutions. Assuring a prisoner that his torture has not broken him, has not made him incapable of forming relationships and functioning in society if he is ever released. Simply listening.

The victories did indeed seem humble when measured against a backdrop of thousands upon thousands of torture sessions. But Pascal and others insisted that these small victories brought incalculable psychic benefits to prisoners. They had seen it. Sometimes it is the change that seems least dramatic, the help that seems most humble, that enables victims engulfed in fear and despair to survive. And, after release, to recover.

Nobody I met at the ICRC seemed troubled by questions of scale. The help such workers give is always small in comparison to the horrors they face. Nevertheless, they all believed firmly that what the ICRC makes possible is a value beyond measure: the emergence of care and the preservation of our small human dignities in worlds of violence and treachery. What *did* trouble Pascal and his colleagues was the possibility that these good intentions might somehow, in some cases, become integrated into the system of treachery itself.

Pascal described to me the case that haunted him the most. It was an instance of psychological rather than physical torture: a prisoner was isolated and, through a variety of indoctrination tactics, forcibly "converted" to a particular sect of Islam. On Pascal's good days, he believes his visits helped because they provided a break for the prisoner, a door to the outside world. On bad days, he wonders if these openings only made the prisoner perceive more keenly the extent of his victimization and degradation. The breaks, as Pascal put it, could have become part of what broke him. "We visit people under interrogation in certain countries after two weeks"—Pascal corrected himself—"We have the *right* to visit them after two weeks. Usually we have the conviction that our visits contribute to an improved psychological state." But, he explained, "we had some doubts at certain points—we made a study about that. People were resilient for two weeks, resistant to interrogation, and then they got a break with the ICRC, which softened them up. And then back to interrogation. It's a hypothesis only, but we had this impression somehow we were integrated in the process in a negative way."

The ICRC was going through a period of internal review when I visited. The organization at that time struck me as uniquely willing to question itself and its assumptions, and Pascal's question went to the very heart of the ICRC. Can the compromises its workers make to gain access make them complicit? The anxiety and depression that affects ICRC delegates is not only the result of "traumatic contagion" and environmental stress. It is the result of a system that requires respecting the confidentiality of executioners, that requires defending the rights of imprisoned génocidaires with the same implacable energy as the rights of rape and torture victims. It is the result of a system that integrates itself into the larger structures of injustice and war that produce the very suffering its workers are dedicated to alleviating.

While in Geneva, I heard many stories. None captured

my feelings about the ICRC's complicated cooperations
with the merchants of violence more succinctly than Brigitte
Troyon's account of her work as a relief worker in Liberia.
She and her staff had food and medicine to deliver, and to
gain access they were willing to work with whomever they
met and to respect the authority of whatever system they
encountered.

"Often you had small boys of seven or eight years man-
ning the checkpoints and wishing to be quite brave," she
began. Her voice was so gentle I at first interpreted it
as timid.

> Children are the most dangerous because they do
> not know that they can die, so they fear nothing. And
> they are trained to kill. They usually had adults be-
> hind them watching them, and they had to prove
> something to these adults. We had, as well, some
> older ones: eighteen, nineteen. They were often high
> on alcohol or drugs.
>
> When we came to the checkpoints, we usually
> tried to avoid defying them. That was a basic rule.
> Try to avoid direct eye contact, as if you are judging
> them, and just agree with them. They want to humil-
> iate you; they want to feel that you are lower than
> they are, so you put yourself in that position. You say,

"I agree with you, I respect what you are saying," and so on.

You had to remain very calm. The children could shoot you without understanding what they were doing. The older ones would sometimes want to keep you as hostage. So you try to calm down the situation and make them see that you appreciate them as human beings. With children, for example, it was quite easy because you just had to play with them. Children there were playing quite easily. So we just mentioned a nice T-shirt they had or nice shoes they had, or we'd say, "How fast can you run?" and things like this. After a while they would even smile at you. They would let you go through if you treated them gently, as children, but at the same time you respected them.

With adults, it was a bit more complicated. We always told them that we respect them. To protect, you need to be able to come again. It's no use coming in and out once, as if then it is finished. You have to build a relationship of trust. So if they tell you to open up the trucks, you do it. If they tell you they want to see things, you let them. It takes time, of course. Once, in the middle of nowhere, they had three checkpoints in ten meters: the so-called

customs, the police, and the army. For a trip that
would take two hours, it took about ten days. But we
worked, and they let us pass.

Philippe Gaillard, head of the ICRC delegation in Rwanda
during the genocide, confirms Troyon's assessment: "Dialogue makes a far better cornerstone for security than armored vehicles or bullet-proof vests. Dialogue is a sign of
openness and trust. An armored vehicle is the physical
expression of fear, withdrawal, and the wrong kind of
strength: aggressive strength."[5]

With such workers and such determination, the ICRC
can reach victims in almost any crisis zone anywhere on
the globe. No other organization has achieved such universal access.

But in Turkey, unlike most countries in the world, the
ICRC was not allowed to pass. Throughout the 1980s and
1990s, its workers were denied access to security detainees
and to civilians affected by the armed conflict with the
Kurdistan Workers Party (PKK) in the southeast of the
country.

After one month in Switzerland, I returned to Ankara.

▮▮▮▮▮ There is no sharper contrast with the communication practices of the ICRC and UNHCR than those of

the Human Rights Association (HRA), which works exclusively in Turkey. The HRA sees itself not as an organization that mediates, judges, or translates the language of the survivor, not as an organization that provides language with specific approved channels, but rather as an organization that is dedicated essentially to the uncontrolled proliferation of survivor language.

Mehmet (not his real name) was the HRA's Speaker for Refugees when I met with him. Mehmet is a young, restlessly energetic, and sleepless man. In my last correspondence with him, he asked to have his identity concealed in this book. As he joked, just because you're paranoid doesn't mean you're not being followed. Although by many accounts Turkey has made significant progress in human rights since I first met Mehmet several years ago, there are still significant risks for workers like him. In 2005, Human Rights Watch sent a letter of concern to the president of Turkey about the HRA. It called for the investigation of death threats made against HRA staff members by shadowy groups with apparent links to the extreme right, noting that "extrajudicial killings and 'disappearances' have claimed the lives of thirteen members of the Human Rights Association over the past fourteen years."[6] That night we first talked years ago, Mehmet smoked ceaselessly and nervously.

Like the ICRC, Mehmet explained, the HRA is involved

in a wide variety of humanitarian and human rights crises, but it is a local, grassroots organization—neither well funded nor well organized. Yet the range of issues it claims to address is startling: torture of prisoners and detainees, extrajudicial killings, censorship of the media and detention of journalists, and forced displacement (hundreds of thousands of Kurds were displaced as a result of the conflict between the Turkish military and the PKK in the 1980s and 1990s). Until recently, the HRA had insufficient capacity to care for refugees and illegal immigrants. But, for Mehmet, such people are a special concern. "The stateless live on the margins of humanity," he says simply. "Indeed, they are outside of humanity. They have no one to help them."

Mehmet is responsible for interviewing refugees and immigrants who claim to have been victims of abuse, and for corroborating their allegations. His job, like Larry's or Pascal's, is to gather information, but his interviews are nothing like those of the UNHCR or ICRC. His first interviews with refugees often occur in their homes, or what are serving as their homes. He is brought to those in hiding by a mutual friend, who usually remains for the interview. Mehmet tells the refugees to say only what they want to say and to stop when they wish, but reminds them that he can be more helpful the more information he receives. "My colleagues are always very compassionate with survivors. Almost everybody involved in our organization was a victim once—torture, detention, rape. We did not join because we were idealists. So the survivors are welcomed as guests, as brothers and sisters." The interviewees often go through multiple sessions. "At some point, they will arrive in our offices. The interviewer himself serves them tea. We don't interrogate them. They are helpless, but when they enter the borders of the Association they become strong. They have a special feeling when they come to our offices."

I asked Mehmet how he was sure he could get accurate information during interviews without replicating the conditions of interrogation that accompanied the original scenes of torture. My time with the UNHCR and the ICRC had convinced me that victims, like anybody else, can exaggerate and lie. How do interviewers balance compassion with accuracy? "In general, our principle is that the survivor in that moment is speaking the truth." The refugee's language is, so to speak, treated as a fact to which people must adapt—a reversal of the process of torture, which, as Elaine Scarry has demonstrated, twists the language of the victim to match the deliberately arbitrary facts of the torturer's world.[7] We do not, Mehmet explained, try to catch them in lies with cross-checking procedures in the interview. And we do not, he stressed, waste much energy eliciting arguments from the "other side." "The statements from the police are always the same: 'This person was not detained.'" But if we wish to take legal action, Mehmet quickly qualified, we must verify our information through any other channel we can use— for instance, by talking to victims' lawyers, doctors, and families.

Unlike the UNHCR, the HRA has no official legitimacy, and on its own can offer nothing more than the promise of voice. What has happened will not be forgotten; what has happened will be reported to somebody, somehow. But in certain cases, with the help of coalitions, the HRA can do more. It is frequently able to mobilize its networks to obtain medical and legal assistance. The work of doctors has been miraculous, and consistently so; the work of lawyers has been astonishing, of late—but this cannot last. In recent years the Council of Europe's Human Rights Court has issued scores of judgments against Turkey for violations[8] (according to Mehmet, the HRA played a key role in some victories). Legal successes here depend, however, upon an unstable conflict of interests in Turkey that must soon be resolved, one way or the other. Turkey's elected political leaders are now caught between the European Union, with its elusive promises of full membership and the economic regeneration this could bring to Turkey, and the powerful military and security forces that operate semi-autonomously in Turkey, unaccountable to the Turkish parliament (according to critics) and unacceptable to Europe because of its alleged systematic human rights violations. Turkey's elected representatives lack both the will and the capacity to challenge the country's army and police, but for now they are also unwilling to cut their ties to the Council of Europe. So they must abide by the decisions of the Human Rights Court as well as the demands of their security forces: as a result, the Turkish government spends significant public funds paying fines and giving court-ordered restitution to its own victims. In Mehmet's words, the government would rather pay for torture than try to prevent it. One activist calls this the torture tax.

Mehmet says Turkey's Ministry of Internal Affairs and National Security Council, citing what are widely perceived as legitimate security concerns in a country long troubled by terrorism, have declared that the Human Rights Association is cooperating with internal and external enemies of the Turkish Republic and is merely disguising itself as a human rights organization. Giving money to the HRA, Mehmet says, was therefore made illegal in Turkey in 1997. The HRA survives by collecting funds

unofficially from its supporters (the HRA claims to have
16,000). Few have anything to give. Excluding a small staff
of administrators, who receive low wages even for Turkey,
the workers are volunteers. Legal and medical work is
pro bono. Mehmet, like many, works full time. He survives
by doing translations in his spare time and receiving help
from his ex-wife, who has also volunteered for the organization. He sums up the difficulties:

> The state operates against us in a variety of ways.
> Their list includes the prevention of field activities
> and missions, prevention of media coverage (which
> is very successful), and distribution of anti–human
> rights propaganda (which is very successful). Many
> of our executive members are or have been impris-
> oned. We have more than 600 court cases against us.
> Every month we pay very high fines to the state.

Lacking official credibility limits the HRA's effectiveness.
Its workers are unable to disseminate information effectively, because of mainstream media blackouts, and for this
reason many Turks—perhaps a majority—are inclined to
accept the government view that the HRA is cooperating
with terrorists. Moreover, because the HRA does not have
a clearly defined public mandate (unlike the UNHCR and

the ICRC, which are, respectively, guardians of the Refugee Convention and the Geneva Conventions), the organization can sometimes suffer from institutional dispersion. In other words, because policy is not constrained by a limited mission, it is also not *focused,* and the consequent uncertainty over the scope and nature of operations can promote infighting and factionalism. By way of example, Mehmet described a running conflict with a disruptive minority in the organization that views the work of human rights as secondary to the goals of a broader, leftist political struggle. The subgroup's insistence that advocacy and resources be distributed according to the dictates of radical politics rather than the principles of human rights has at times threatened to fracture the organization.

As this case shows in a negative way, the HRA's official illegitimacy can also be the source of a powerful freedom. At the ICRC and UNHCR, humanitarian work is defined by its limits: workers must accept that they can help only a certain kind of victim; they must accept that war and government detentions can be only ameliorated, not eliminated. HRA volunteers have accepted no such limits. They are not aiming to adjudicate the distribution of a scarce resource, like Seda Kuzucu, or to reduce the barbarism of barbaric situations, like Pascal Daudin. Their goal is to bring about the transformation of the regime, case by

:, according to the principle that a state's existence is ified *only* as the guarantor of human rights.

HRA volunteers need make no moral compromises to protect their public image, to guarantee access, or to respect a limited mandate. They have no public image, and their mandate, if it can be called that, is to help anyone in any way they can. They do not need to protect the confidentiality of inhumane authority or sift through the deceit of abusive security forces in their search for an inclusive truth; the ICRC's struggle to remain neutral is alien to them. They do not need to exclude some victims in order to uphold a legal standard; the UNHCR's struggle to remain objective is alien to them. HRA volunteers are not neutral and not objective. They are partisans. In most cases they are survivors of the very abuses they are now fighting; and having once before crouched beneath the blows of police batons, they live each day with the promise that they will never again bow to the force of the state. Brigitte Troyon's painstaking deference to local authority is as inconceivable for them as courtesy to a fist.

In the end, HRA partisanship affects not only how survivors are interviewed but also how their stories are translated to the outside world. Whereas the goal of the UNHCR is to achieve an evidentiary threshold and sustain legal legitimacy through descriptive precision, the HRA's primary

goal is to achieve persuasion and sustain emotional commitment through dramatic, morally coercive descriptions
(the ICRC fits somewhere in between, depending upon the
local context). It should be noted that the language work
of each of these three organizations, consequently, has not
only a different level of moral complexity but also a different power capacity.

The spectrum starts at one extreme with the maximally
effective UNHCR, where legitimacy derived from the rule
of law makes UNHCR communications into textbook examples of speech acts: in other words, saying "You are a
refugee" is equivalent to the act of making the person
a refugee—or, more accurately, making the person into
somebody the UN recognizes as a refugee, with all the
protections this entails.

The middle range is occupied by the ICRC. Because the
norms of international humanitarian law (IHL) function
more like moral claims than like enforceable law, ICRC
declarations are speech acts only in the way all utterances
are speech acts. That is, saying "You are violating IHL"
does not make that person into a criminal officially; but
because the utterance is preceded implicitly by the phrase
"We state that," then it *is* true that the utterance makes
it the case that somebody is being officially condemned
by the ICRC. And this carries some normative weight,

both for the security forces thus condemned, given that their supervising officials have bestowed legitimacy upon the ICRC by granting them access, and also for the state itself, given that most nations have consented to the Geneva Conventions or to similar moral and legal norms.

At the other extreme is the HRA, whose utterances have neither official internal legitimacy nor normative weight, except for what it can borrow from other international organizations. As a consequence, the HRA attempts to give its utterances weight and to attract international attention to its utterances through sheer force of language. Rhetorical practice, in other words, is in large part a product of organizational capacity.

Unsurprisingly, for many years HRA press releases against the government were relentless, severe, and sometimes reckless. HRA personnel made little effort to temper their rhetoric and sometimes failed to make distinctions between allegations and facts. And they offered their information to any organization they could reach, from local groups to international media outlets and nongovernmental organizations, without worrying that they might thus jeopardize their ability to gather information in the future. Their work was both a form of release and revenge, and an experiment in the power of shaming. The effectiveness of this aggressive strategy remains uncertain.

Mehmet, for one, was skeptical. "The focus on international criticism was counterproductive. The more the international community criticized Turkey for gross violations, the more the Turkish politicians, the media, and
increasingly the civil society adopted a defensive national-
ist position." For many citizens, he explained, patriotism
became intertwined with support of the embattled security forces. All our talk, he said, may only have given a
cloak to the torture. Like Seda and Pascal, Mehmet had begun to formulate his mission as a psychically crippling double-bind: the more aggressively we work to protect the individual, the worse it might be for the whole over time.
Mehmet emphasized that the HRA, as a result, had recently begun to try to change its tactics, and perhaps un-
intentionally he quoted words I had often heard from the
Red Cross. "Our job is not to condemn human rights violations. It is to prevent violations before they happen. So a
rhetoric which is more careful, more diplomatic, more
constructive, more positive—this would make the authorities more cooperative." With cooperation from authorities, Mehmet explained, the HRA might be able to reach
detainees, to protect them. At the moment, however, the
mutual hostility was too extreme. It would have been unimaginable, for instance, for members of the HRA to meet
with paramilitary forces to educate them on humane

tactics of detention, or to negotiate with their contacts among police officers to obtain access to or release of prisoners. The HRA had no contacts, only enemies.

It was late at night when we finished our interview. During our hours together, Mehmet's accounts of police and paramilitary torture and killings had accumulated like thick smoke in the air. By 2:00 A.M. I was exhausted, but Mehmet was still full of nervous energy; he had a number of calls to return and documents to prepare, and would get only a few hours' sleep before taking an early-morning flight to Istanbul. I asked him what kept him going. Like the UNHCR officers, he listed cigarettes, alcohol, and sex. Then he added one more item: anger.

Tomorrow was a fresh outrage. Mehmet was flying to Istanbul to investigate allegations that a group of Africans who had entered the country illegally and not received refugee status had been tortured by the police and abandoned, disabled and starving, in a remote border zone. Denied entry into the neighboring country, the victims had struggled to find their way back to Istanbul and had gone into hiding. Mehmet had seen many such crises. "It is arbitrary and illegal," he said, finishing his last cigarette. "But the police do it to thousands of immigrants and refugees a year. Those not under the protection of the

UNHCR are especially vulnerable." Mehmet, for once, showed fatigue.

I had been in Turkey one month. The stories were endless. I asked Mehmet if he had any hope.

"Of course I have hope," he said, without hesitation. "I have hope because I am working."

BURNOUT

There is no reliable, comprehensive data on deaths among humanitarian workers, but much of the available information points to a steady rise in fatalities—presumably because humanitarian relief is increasingly directed not toward wars between states but rather toward internal conflicts in weak or failed states, where civilians and those protecting them are often direct targets.[1] While death is still not a common outcome in humanitarian work, exposure to the risk of death is.

Colleen Striegel, director of human resources for the American Refugee Committee (ARC), says that heightened risks and associated stress have made it increasingly difficult to recruit and retain workers in recent years. Particularly in smaller organizations, she claims, many burn out in the first couple of years.

Chantal Lebrat was a delegate for the ICRC and the Or-

ganization for Security and Cooperation in Europe, serving with missions in Bosnia, Armenia, Chechnya, Russia,
and Kosovo. When asked about the primary stressor in humanitarian work, she replied: "At first, it's the idea of dying. But you are also afraid of the unpredictable. If you get
used to gunfire starting up every evening at 19:00, you will
be afraid if the town stays quiet. But it can also be hilari-
ous. I remember one day when a colleague in charge of aid
started counting us to see if there were enough body-bags
in stock."[2]

Kenneth Cain served with UN missions throughout the
1990s, in countries ranging from Cambodia to Rwanda.
The work began for him as an inescapable moral call, but
he quit, finally, while on mission in Liberia. He left for
many reasons (his career ended with a sickening jolt that
I will discuss toward the end of this chapter), but key
among these was the simple and continual pressure of fear.
"Once you've nominated yourself as the person who has
the courage to do this, you've trapped yourself—because
when you stop, that means you're the person who's now
afraid to do this. That's hard. But at the end of it I was
afraid, for sure. I kind of lost my nerve. I started to feel like
I had nine lives and I was on my eighth. Like, one more
bad checkpoint, you know?" Cain is quite open about the
mental and emotional problems the work has caused. He

drank heavily for a time, suffered from vivid nightmares, and still has difficulty with panic reactions. Back home in the States, he's been haunted by the image of the bodies from Rwanda. "In the subway in the summer, the urine-and-garbage smell is really close to a rotting-body smell. And that sends me to a bad place." Group therapy with his colleagues has helped.

In the college where I teach, getting involved in humanitarian and human rights work is increasingly one of the most popular stated ambitions of students.[3] The risks of the work have not seemed to dishearten my students—on the contrary, risk seems part of what makes it attractive to them, part of what enchants them. In this chapter, I would like to examine the nature of such enchantment. Why do people seek out this kind of service? What attracts them to it, what rewards keep them there, and what, in the end, may drive them away? The answers to these questions reveal much, not only about the psychology of human rights, but also about the nature of moral motivation itself.

I

In *The Republic,* Plato discusses our attraction to the sight of human suffering: "The story is that Leontius, the son of Aglaion, coming up one day from the Piraeus, under the north wall on the outside, observed some dead bodies ly-

ing on the ground at the place of execution. He felt a desire to see them, and also a dread and abhorrence of them;
for a time he struggled and covered his eyes, but at length
the desire got the better of him; and forcing them open, he
ran up to the dead bodies, saying, Look, ye wretches, take
your fill of the fair sight."[4]

What pulls you? What is your motivation? It is a question asked frequently of people involved in humanitarian
work. It is a question they frequently ask themselves. At
the Museum of the International Red Cross in Geneva in
2004–2005, an exhibition was dedicated to the question,
"Why do people nowadays commit themselves to humanitarian action?"[5] Some wish to know because they have
felt called to act but never did, and they believe that, by
coming to understand those who volunteered, they might
thereby understand what was lacking in themselves. Others are curious to know, really know, because they admire
the commitment, but also because they resist what seems
to be its demand for admiration—because the choice to do
the work seems to contain within it an implicit judgment
of those who do not. And for the workers themselves it
can be an urgent question because the primary motivations for the work are sometimes, as we shall see, the very
things that render people unfit for it.

Many fieldworkers, when talking about their occupation, characterize it in Plato's terms: as a pleasure that co-erces. "It's a bit of an addiction," says one of the charac-ters—a humanitarian worker—in Alan Cumyn's powerful human rights novel *Burridge Unbound*. "The next crisis. All that adrenaline, it's a real high until you crash."[6] This lan-guage of addiction is prevalent among aid workers. After the first mission, you have to find another, and another. Heidi Postlewait, describing the work she did supervis-ing Cambodia's first elections in 1993, expresses an in-discriminate hunger that is typical: "The election is over. Cambodians are on their own. But I'm not getting back on the Staten Island Ferry. There must be another election or landslide or war somewhere where UN secretaries are needed."[7]

The best analogy for this need came to me from some-body who was an ex-smoker, describing what it felt like to have a cigarette in the days before he kicked the habit. He put it this way: Life is full of "good enough." We have all sorts of needs and all sorts of ways of more or less meet-ing them. But according to him, anyway, nothing we get ever matches a need perfectly—no meal, no aesthetic de-light, no sexual encounter—at least, not in the way having a cigarette did for him. That satisfaction was total, clean, whole, each time. It required no adaptation; it left no re-mainder. Like (his metaphor) the feeling of finally urinating when the release has been long delayed. And remember, he emphasized, that I'm talking about *sensual* needs, which are always more easy to satisfy than moral or emotional needs. Most of us live lives that are defined in part, or in key moments, by the aching experience of seeing others in the grip of physical need or emotional pain and finding ourselves totally incapable of helping. Most of our lives are lived in deep moral frustration in that sense, in what amounts to a deep craving. When this is satisfied even for a moment, the relief physically hits us, by this man's metaphor, like the pleasure of gratifying an addiction.

"The work is addictive," agrees Kenneth Cain.[8] The accounts of nearly every humanitarian worker I've spoken with echo this. So many are able to recall that dizzying moment when, perhaps for the first time in their lives, they were able to match somebody's moral need perfectly, to close the gap of the other's pain with simple totality. It is, inevitably, depressing and traumatic, and also one of the loveliest things that will ever happen to them. When I asked Kenneth Cain what he found most rewarding about his years in the field, he told me about his triage work in Rwanda after the massacre at Kibeho in 1995. There were thousands and thousands of Rwandans—dehydrated, unconscious, dying—who had fled to the bottom of the mountain and gathered around the few small medical tents that relief workers had put together. The doctors in the tents were too busy with patients to survey the wounded outside and make triage decisions, so they sent Cain. He had no medical experience.

> So I ended up choosing kids because that seemed to be—I don't know why, but that's what I chose. So if you're the white guy in a sea of ten thousand Africans who comes and takes a baby and brings it to the doctor—you know, you do that once and you're identified as the guy who comes and saves your baby's life, right? So I brought one kid in. The next time I go out I'm just surrounded by mothers with kids who are hurt. They're just kind of throwing their babies at me—this one has a machete wound, and this one has gunk here, and this one's bleeding—it was a living nightmare.

Cain soon realized that the ones he could save most quickly were the dehydrated babies. Against every traumatic memory that resurges for Cain stands the memory of what happened next. "The kid goes from next-to-dead—you know, they have really clammy skin, they have this weird pallor, they're going to die—and they pump this saline solution in and the kid literally just comes to life. The eyes open, the skin starts to change, and then they start looking around and they're a hundred percent okay." In a tent for the wounded and dying, now there were infants wanting to play. "I would watch them come to life," he said. "Just by your sheer physical presence you're able to save lives, with your hands." Telling me the story almost a decade later, he sounded as if he still couldn't believe it. Moments like that, he said—that's what makes it addictive.

But altruism invites scrutiny. In Helen Fielding's novel *Cause Celeb*—a comic sendup of the humanitarian community, based on her experience making documentaries in Sudan and Ethiopia for a fundraising program—one of the characters wears a T-shirt designed to look like a multiple-choice questionnaire for relief workers. It reads:

(a) Missionary?

(b) Mercenary?

(c) Misfit?

(d) Broken heart?[9]

Later in the novel, a fifth option is revealed: ennui. "I'm really bored with my life, you know?" one of her privileged minor characters laments, studying images of starving Africans. "I really want to change my life. This feels

real to me, you know?"[10] Mark Jacobs, a writer who served
in the Peace Corps in Paraguay, depicts the centrality of
self in selfless work this way in his fiction: "She finally
knew why she was in Paraguay. . . . That political stuff
didn't interest her the way she thought it should, though
she had tried. . . . She was there to become someone she
could not be in Gasport, New York, in the company
of carping aunts."[11] Deborah Scroggins, writing of relief
work in Sudan, explains that "what was tedious for the refugees could be exciting for expatriates": "Here as in the
rest of Africa, *khawajas* [white Westerners] were forever
turning to one another to say, with pleased surprise, 'Did
you know my brother is a stockbroker?'—and then smiling
in mutual satisfaction for having escaped such a fate."[12]

The disconcerting paradox of humanitarian work is this:
it is sometimes impossible to distinguish the desire to help
others from the desire to amplify the self, to distinguish
altruism from narcissism. Clea Koff told me that she
stopped working for the United Nations criminal tribunals
in part because she found herself working more and more
with forensic pathologists who came to the mass graves
because it was "sexy" and (since the pathologists could, in
this way, see an extraordinary number of cases on their va-
cation time) professionally advantageous. Even Kenneth
Cain's story of revivified children can be read—and Cain

would be the first to admit this—not as the experience of moral relief but as the intoxicating experience of power. Indeed, the book that Cain wrote with his colleagues Heidi Postlewait and Andrew Thomson, *Emergency Sex and Other Desperate Measures*—an account of their years working in the field for the UN—reads much like Jack Kerouac's exuberant novel of self-exploration, *On the Road:*

> The water starts to form waves in rhythm with the beat of our thrusts and the Swiss girl is beautiful and the pot and rum and music are in charge and then a giant wave forms from a group hip thrust executed in perfect unison and it crashes out of the pool and washes over in a small tidal wave all the way to the electric cable spliced from the generator that's feeding the blender and boom box and everyone stops and waits to die and nothing happens and we're young and immortal and together and drunk and stupid and in Cambodia.[13]

As David Rieff writes: "At least for anyone over thirty-five, it is the youth of most aid workers in the field that is immediately striking."[14]

When the protagonist of *Cause Celeb* takes a dangerous journey through a war zone as part of a mission to bring

aid to suffering refugees, she notes: "There are few real
adventures to be had in the modern world and this was a
real adventure. We were being as self-indulgent as brave."[15]
For Fielding, as for Cain, there is something troubling about
achieving fulfillment through acts of selflessness. You can
never truly know your own motivations, much less the
motivations of others, and it is always possible that
selflessness per se is what you wish to achieve. In other
words, you are enchanted by an image of yourself as
selfless; the human material that allows you to generate
that image is secondary. The fact that narcissism motivates
people's work is, in most cases, untroubling. But it troubles
here, because our failure to find a fundamental altruism in
this of all places suggests we'll never find it anywhere. The
gap that separates us from our ideals can inspire the most
cynical self-conceptions. "UN general, BBC correspondent,
aid worker, mercenary," war correspondent Anthony Loyd
writes. "In the final analysis they all want the same thing: a
hit off the action, a walk on the dark side. It's just a question of how slick a cover you give yourself."[16]

But self-serving motives in this work are troubling, above
all, because of the terrible vulnerability of the people for
whom the "adventures" are undertaken. Speaking of the
crucial motivation letter required of all applicants to the
ICRC, Marco Yuri Jiménez Rodríguez, ICRC spokesperson

for Africa, says ego is "dangerous" for humanitarian organizations. Though this isn't the rule, it can happen that
some individuals seeking the work may be driven by the
desire to feel "important and powerful." "In the field, some
people can be tempted to be something like a king," he
says, "because of the relative power people have in front
of those around so vulnerable." Philip Gourevitch offers
an extreme example of the cruelty of such narcissism:
"You know the story, right? I think it was in the Congo in
the Fifties or early Sixties, and there had been some nuns
raped, and there was a journalist on deadline who went
to the camp where these victims of this massacre and pil-
lage and violation had taken place. And he went walking through, saying, 'Anyone here been raped who speaks
English?'"

   "I have a lot of personal affection and respect and admiration for a number of people who do humanitarian
work," Gourevitch said. "I'm wary when it is a comfortable, bureaucratic lifestyle that involves a certain amount
of exotic adventure and gives you access to a very high
level of self-congratulation. But I'm most wary," he continued with emphasis, "of the notion that at any given moment we know what's best for everybody else. The question is, are you doing this out of a real considered and
understood sense of the situation in which you're acting,

or are you having a parasitic relationship to other people's misfortunes and difficulties because your own life feels sort of without edges and without friction and without tests?" If it is the latter, he said, you run a high risk of hurting rather than helping.

Michael Ignatieff, formerly the director of the Carr Center for Human Rights Policy at Harvard University and now a member of the Canadian parliament, put it the following way when we talked about the idea behind his book *Charlie Johnson in the Flames* (a novel about bearing witness to atrocity). Sometimes "extreme forms of moral certainty are a desperate attempt to fill another, much deeper spiritual vacuum in the center." There are real "dangers," he said, to this "intoxication of strong moral feeling"—there are, often, "catastrophic consequences to such good intentions." "I spend my career teaching young people to have good intentions," he says, "and then I spend the second half of my time teaching about the dangers and unintended consequences of good intentions."

Kenneth Cain puts it in stronger terms:

> If you don't recognize the narcissism of the endeavor, you're inevitably guaranteeing blindness. It's the narcissism of righteousness. It's obviously true that the self is forefront in this endeavor. I think it's healthy to

recognize that, because then you can understand
your blindness and correct it. Somalia is a great example. The mission was—it was called "Restore
Hope," we were going to recreate a government.
That was what we had in our head. When we landed
on the ground, however, the people who lived there
didn't see it that way. They saw it as an invasion.
That's not complicated—but if you're blinded by your
righteousness and your narcissism, you either don't
see it or you can't see it or you deny it. We forgot
to tell the Somalis how righteous we are. And they
kicked us out, and I think that has had disastrous consequences in Rwanda, Bosnia, and Iraq.

What pulls you? What is your motivation? In his book,
Cain recalls how he was inspired by a young South African—a conscientious objector just released from prison—
who said, referring to the Holocaust: "I have to show by
my actions that if I had been a German citizen, I would
have risked my life and fought the regime; I am a hypocrite
if my action does not match my belief."[17] Yes, it was that,
and it was something else. As Cain told me: "It was a thrill,
a big thrill. You're on a business-class plane all over the
world; you have a diplomatic passport. It was the early
Nineties, so the UN was seen as this great force of hope.

It was really heady, and it was really fun, and we were young, Clinton was young, peacekeeping was young, everybody was young, everybody was beautiful. You enter an international scene for the first time, and it's sexually charged—people dress differently, and smell differently, and dance differently. It's exciting as hell, especially when you're young."

II

Elie Wiesel calls human rights norms a "world-wide secular religion." Upendra Baxi writes that the language of human rights has emerged as "the only universal ideology in the making, enabling both the legitimation of power and the *praxis* of emancipatory politics." And Michael Ignatieff, tracking what he calls the post–World War II "international rights revolution," argues that human rights discourse "has become the lingua franca of global moral thought."[18]

Robin Phillips, executive director of Minnesota Advocates for Human Rights, explains how this celebrated but sometimes abstract idea of a moral consensus can reach hearts and minds in simple but powerful ways. She recalls interviewing an official in the Ministry of Internal Affairs in Moldova, who told her how demoralized he had been when he was assigned to head the domestic-violence unit. It didn't feel like real police work, he said. But when his superiors told him that Moldova had to comply with international human rights standards and that the United Nations had stated unequivocally that violence against women, including domestic violence, violated the fundamental human rights of women, he began to experience what can only be described as a personal transformation. "It changed him," Phillips says. The official began to think of himself as a defender of human rights. "It gave him inspiration to do his job, to do it differently, to do it with pride and I think greater vigor."

The accumulating moral force of rights-language is both the cause and result of an almost unprecedented institutional explosion, from monumental international declarations like the Universal Declaration of Human Rights (1948) to the ad hoc criminal tribunals (Nuremberg, Tokyo, the former Yugoslavia, Rwanda) that have culminated in the permanent International Criminal Court. Prior to World War II, Johannes Morsink writes, there were "almost no international instruments concerned with the realization of human rights"; but by the fiftieth anniversary of the Universal Declaration of Human Rights, there were "around 200 assorted declarations, conventions, protocols, treaties, charters, and agreements."[19] Law professor David Weissbrodt, who served as a member and also chairperson of the UN Subcommission on the Promotion and Protec-

tion of Human Rights, put it to me this way in an exchange about the disputed force of these instruments: "We
can compare the progress of international human rights
law with improvements in civil liberties and civil rights
law in the United States. A century or more ago the judicial and practical impact of the US Bill of Rights and similar provisions in state constitutions was minimal. It has
taken more than two centuries to develop effective legal
protections for the rights of US residents and train lawyers
how to protect those rights. By comparison, international
human rights law has developed with impressive speed."

The pace of development on the nongovernmental side
is equally remarkable. In the years 1953–1993, transnational
advocacy networks working in human rights quintupled in
number, from 33 to 168. To give a sense of the dramatic
changes in the "speed, density, and complexity of international linkages among them," Margaret Keck and Kathryn
Sikkink borrow a metaphor from a study of domestic political networks: "If the current situation is a mere out-
growth of old tendencies, it is so in the same sense that a
sixteen-lane spaghetti interchange is a mere elaboration of
a country crossroads."[20]

Here is just one example of the proliferation. In the fall
of 2004, the Center for Victims of Torture (CVT), based in
Minneapolis, Minnesota (the first comprehensive torture
treatment center in the United States), organized an inter-

national workshop in Ankara, Turkey, that brought together approximately 450 human rights activists from 89
countries to share tactical innovations that would improve
strategies for advancing human rights. Case studies ranged
from campaigns to defend Colombian refugees in Vene-
zuela and reforming the judicial system in Uzbekistan, to
working for sustainable development in Nigeria and promoting ethical investments in the United States. Douglas
Johnson, executive director of the center, looks to a future
field that is even more densely integrated and increasingly
wide in its reach, encompassing economic, social, and cultural rights: "Advancing human rights requires the creation
of a broader human rights field, one that incorporates
many more people and sectors of society than are currently engaged. It also requires the development of more
comprehensive strategic approaches that can only be accomplished by using a far broader array of tactics than are
currently in use."

With this rise of a global human rights infrastructure
has come a burgeoning sense of ambition and hope. William Schulz, executive director of Amnesty International
USA, emphasized to me the dramatic changes that have
taken place in little more than a decade:

> We've seen the creation of the International Crimi-
> nal Court; we've seen rape defined as a war crime;

we've seen the enormous growth of indigenous human rights organizations in even some of the most
repressive countries in the world; we've seen
Milosevic in the dock at the Hague. . . . [In the United
States] the Supreme Court in the last six years has
ruled unconstitutional both the execution of juve-
niles and of the mentally retarded, and done so on
two almost revolutionary grounds. First, in part, on
the basis of international law, which the court has
rarely cited. And second, on the basis of evolving
community standards, meaning that grassroots people actually did have an impact on changing the laws
in enough states to convince the Supreme Court that
the definition of cruel and unusual punishment had
evolved. That's a significant victory.

But with all such accomplishments and the aspirations they
generate, there are also failures and, consequently, sharp
disillusionment. Kenneth Cain's book is one of many
that might be called dissident works of the human rights
movement, including Upendra Baxi's *The Future of Human
Rights,* David Kennedy's *The Dark Sides of Virtue: Reassessing International Humanitarianism,* Makau Mutua's *Human Rights: A Political and Cultural Critique,* and David
Rieff's *A Bed for the Night: Humanitarianism in Crisis.*[21] Baxi

warns, among other things, that institutionalizing human rights can be a way of defanging it. He argues that the proliferation of nongovernmental organizations (NGOs) and their participation in larger organizational structures (global NGO networks, conferences, and summits; integration into the United Nations and state governments) has led to an "enfeeblement of the potential of forms of creative antagonism into hurried and harried postures of compromise and cooperation." Moreover, "the production of an international agenda for human rights is increasingly marked by a dominant concern to make the 'civil society' a co-equal partner," with the result that "corporations and other economic entities are equal partners to human rights realization." In other words, "the paradigm of the Universal Declaration of Human Rights is being steadily, but surely, *supplanted* by that of a trade-related, market-friendly human rights," leading to *"the privatization of the United Nations"* itself.[22]

In his wide-ranging critique, David Kennedy catalogues a series of potentially negative consequences of the human rights movement—from the justification of irresponsible interventions to the privileging of civil and political rights over social and economic rights (as Johnson's comment and the CVT symposium reveal, however, this latter tendency is changing: Amnesty International, for example,

recently expanded its mandate to include defending economic, social, and cultural rights).[23] Kennedy also asserts
that the "institutional and political hegemony" of human
rights draws energy, workers, and resources away from
"other valuable, often more valuable, emancipatory strategies."[24] As he put it when we spoke: "There certainly are
other emancipatory rhetorics in the world that have been
invented and have not been as well funded. Look at Catho-
lic social charities; look at a variety of different religious
movements; look at the now moribund labor movement.
Without this globally validated and often lavishly funded
human rights movement, might people have invented
something different?" When I asked how he would respond to those who argue that a comparative criticism
based on unidentified alternatives cannot stand, he said:
"It doesn't seem to be any critique of the argument to
say that I don't know what it is, because by definition I
don't know what it is." Indeed, as he writes in his book, the
difficulty in elaborating what these "other ways of understanding harm and recompense" might be is itself evidence of the stultifying dominance of human rights: "Alternatives can now be thought only, perhaps unhelpfully, as
negations of what human rights asserts—passion to its reason, local to its global."[25]

Kennedy's critique-by-alternative overlaps, I believe, with

the work of Makau Mutua and others, who argue that the global human rights movement is fundamentally defined by a Eurocentric bias, protecting "norms and practices that may be detrimental to societies in the Third World." Mutua explains:

> In the West, the language of rights primarily developed along the trajectory of claims against the state: entitlements which imply the right to seek an individual remedy for a wrong. The African language of duty, however, offers a different meaning for individual / state-society relations: while people had rights, they also bore duties. The resolution of a claim was not necessarily directed at satisfying or remedying an individual wrong. It was an opportunity for society to contemplate the complex web of individual and community duties and rights to seek a balance between the competing claims of the individual and the society.[26]

Hauwa Ibrahim is a Nigerian human rights advocate and lawyer who became the focus of worldwide attention in 2003 when she successfully defended Amina Lawal in the Sharia Court of Appeal of Katsina, Nigeria, overturning Lawal's sentence of stoning to death for adultery. Ibrahim addressed this issue of cultural difference when we spoke. She emphasized, first, that in her work defending poor Nigerians from the harshest punishments of the Sharia courts, "international human rights documentation . . . is extremely relevant." We read these declarations, cases, and reports and ask: "How can we apply the same principle, but using our local circumstances to apply the principle? . . . The fact that we have those instruments that are there and being used in your own different communities and societies—it has been really a huge success to us in understanding how it's being used and to apply it locally. So, yes, we need them." That said, however, people in the United States "can talk with some kind of confidence and some kind of relaxation about human rights, [but] in a lot of other places they are only words." She recalled work she had done in a village attempting to introduce microcredit and literacy programs. When she emphasized to the women there that being able to read and write would help them to know their rights, "the women asked us to get out. They said they don't want to know their rights as far as they're concerned because they're happy with their husband and their children." They would participate in the loan programs, "but they don't want to know anything about rights." When you use the words of human rights, she concluded, their success "depends on what setting you use them [in]. They may not carry any meaning." And if they do carry meaning, it may be very different from what you intend.[27]

David Rieff sets out another important critique. In *A Bed for the Night,* he maintains that the increasing politicization of humanitarian intervention has made it a supplement of national foreign policies, a justification for and extension of new imperialisms. "By the time of the Bosnian crisis," he writes, humanitarian workers had become "an instrument and emblem of the reach and power of Western governments."[28]

Karen Elshazly, Senior Advisor to the President of the American Refugee Committee, knows this from firsthand experience. Her organization was among the first to deliver medical supplies to the Middle East after the second Gulf War. "The military wanted to go with us, mainly for public relations," she told me. She was "very uncomfortable" over integrating with the military. The ARC, moreover, felt it was unnecessary: they had established relationships and knew the safe routes—but, as she put it carefully, "we were unable to say no." "In places like Iraq and Afghanistan," she says, "it just becomes very much married to the military agenda. . . . It gets really mixed up." One day you're retaliating with lethal force; the next day, in the same area, you're delivering medical supplies. It's danger-ously confusing, she says, for both peacekeeper and population. Hence the neologism "intravasion"—a barbed renaming that novelist Nuruddin Farah applies to the US humanitarian intervention in Somalia.[29]

James Guy, a clinical psychologist specializing in counseling and care for humanitarian workers, believes this blending of missions is a problem that reaches all the way into the therapy process. "Where does aid start and stop, and where does control take over?" he asks. "There's been a pairing of humanitarian aid with political control and military coercion in a way that's just so much more prominent than in the past." He cites accounts "from people on the inside who are just so angry, just so disillusioned about that." Many, in fact, fear that such "integrated" missions are the way of the future—and, relatedly, that in places where care is needed, traditional nonprofit humanitarian organizations will be displaced by corporations with a profit motive (like the companies sent to Iraq when the US occupation began).[30]

In such a context, all intervention becomes suspect. In his novel *Gifts*, Nuruddin Farah offers depictions of aid as a straightforward, even intentional harm. "Unasked-for generosity has a way of making one feel obliged, trapped in a labyrinth of dependence," the protagonist Duniya says. "Haven't we in the Third World lost our self-reliance and pride because of the so-called aid we unquestioningly receive from the so-called First World?" The story includes discussion of how "foreign food donations create a buffer zone between corrupt leaderships and the starving masses," how the European Community sends to Somalia butter and milk that have been contaminated by radiation from Chernobyl, and how leaders in the West use giving "to dominate." In the novel, US statesman Hubert Humphrey says: "I've heard . . . that people may become dependent on us for food. I know this is not supposed to be good news. To me that was good news, because before people can do anything, they have got to eat. And if you're looking for a way to get people to lean on you and to be dependent on you, in terms of their co-operation with you, it seems to me food dependence would be terrific."[31]

Destination Biafra, by Buchi Emecheta, presents a similarly shameful situation. The aid described here might be less blameworthy in its effects, but it is more so in its motives. The British who assist the Red Cross and politically intervene to stop genocide in Nigeria do so only at the very end, as a sop to conscience, after arranging the hiring of mercenaries and profitable arms sales that sustained the slaughter.

In yet another perspective on the hurtfulness of aid, Hauwa Ibrahim explained to me how secretaries in offices for development programs sometimes work secretly as informants for groups interested in poaching international funding. They release information about upcoming initiatives so that their contacts can "incorporate an NGO that will reflect what the project is all about. So all of a sudden you have 'mushrooms,' NGOs coming up, and they're taking all the jobs. I mean everything that comes will never go anywhere." She said with passion:

> If people will give money and they cannot follow up about accountability, I will say—with huge respect—please don't give the money! We don't need it. It's spoiling the entire system that we're trying to build. The lack of transparency and accountability is not good, but it's even worse when donors just give funding and think that it will work out. I think there must be very close monitoring, and they must please hold on to their money until they know they can have creative ways . . . of monitoring how their funds have been used. I do not think we need any more money that will corrupt us more, or will corrupt our system, our values, or our setting.

As a character from Ken Saro-Wiwa's short story "Night Ride" puts it, "I fear the Greeks and the gifts they bring."[32]

In the United States, Kenneth Cain was, for a few years, one of the most highly visible of the many public critics of human rights and humanitarian endeavors. His bitter disillusionment with his career, his experience of turning his back on the dreams of his youth, reproduces at the level of intimate psychology the broader intellectual and policy volte-faces against human rights culture represented in the work of people like Mutua, Kennedy, Baxi, and Rieff. Like them, Cain has larger policy recommendations; but I would like to focus on his career affect and on the causes of his burnout, as a way of opening up other, more personal questions about the ways we may find ourselves unfitted for the work and, therefore, ineffective and disenchanted. Cain's disenchantment with the United Nations, human rights norms, and humanitarianism in general is indeed extreme—as extreme as his early idealism. "The people who benefit the most from the human rights movement are the people in the human rights movement," he told me bluntly. "The amount of energy, time, and hope invested is massively disproportional to the amount of concrete good that's effected." It breaks his heart, he said, that the good is such a shadow of what it could be.

In *Achilles in Vietnam,* a powerful examination of the unique psychological challenges faced by veterans of the Vietnam War, psychiatrist Jonathan Shay argues that one of the primary reasons combat trauma symptoms were so pernicious for these men was the pervasiveness of what he called "moral injury."[33] All wars are defined by fear, injury, and terrible loss, but when this is accompanied by a sense that one has been betrayed or shamed, a sense that those in charge have violated "what's right," the psychological injury is radically amplified. If we cannot tell ourselves a story about our experience and the larger endeavor that feels honorable, we are rendered psychologically vulnerable. Pride—it turns out—can actually help us to recover from traumatic stressors.

After my interview with Cain, we shared a taxi ride together to the UN headquarters in New York, where—despite his liberal political commitments—Cain was participating in a right-wing documentary attacking the institution. When I mentioned that I thought Jonathan Shay's work on war veterans might be relevant to him, he nodded vigorously. What had made Cain feel like he couldn't go on? What had rattled him, made him feel like he wasn't doing any good? Cain alleges that UN peacekeeping forces have committed serious crimes against those they are charged to protect. He also maintains that in Liberia, local staff, desperately vulnerable because of their poverty, were being coerced into sex by a UN employee he knew. Cain says that when he reported this to higher authorities at the

UN, they laughed at him, saying: "Do you know how many allegations like this we get? We can't possibly investigate them all." Cain quit that very day.

It seemed clear to me as I spoke with Cain that this experience was heartbreaking and shaming for him in and of itself, but that also, on some level, it reproduced in him the sense of betrayal he carried about Rwanda: people like us are trying to do what's right on the front lines and our officers are abandoning us; they aren't doing what's right, and we have to clean up afterwards. Earlier in the day Cain had told me that one of the hardest things for him since leaving the field was riding in taxicabs. He would often panic and become enraged—he attributed this to his traumatic experiences in convoys in active war zones. This is how he put it: he cannot stand it when incompetent people are driving his bus.

Colleen Striegel cites a 2002 fact-finding mission that reported widespread sexual exploitation in refugee camps; as a result of the findings, her organization helped establish a legal clinic in Guinea, the first of its kind linked to a refugee camp, to help survivors prosecute aid workers and other perpetrators of gender-based violence. In an internal report on the legal aid project, the American Refugee Committee notes that many "cases of exploitation seemed to involve NGO and UNHCR aid workers and Guinean government employees who used their position of power and authority and their money to lure refugee minors into sexual relations with the express or implied promise of caring for them by providing them with food, clothing, shoes, etc. However, once the girls become pregnant, they are abandoned, which typically leads them to the life of a commercial sex worker."

Anger over such betrayals changes everything for Kenneth Cain. In the end, he believes his years in the field added no net good to the world. According to his friend and colleague Heidi Postlewait, the inner idealism that drove Cain to do the work proved, in this way, to be one of his greatest handicaps. "I never went into this with these grand ideas of changing the world," she says. "I think I was more patient and realistic, and it was difficult for me to listen to the two of them [Cain and Thomson] think that, you know, in the one- or two-year mandate of a mission, that everything could come about and be peaceful and democratic. I just thought that was foolish. So, yeah, I often became impatient with them." She continues: "I thought that they were naïve, and I think what happened is I wasn't let down as much as them at the end of our missions."[34]

Mark Brayne, a psychotherapist who is the director for European operations at the Dart Center for Journalism

and Trauma, emphasizes that many professionals working regularly in war zones and other areas of calamity find
psychological balance only through the de-escalation of
hopes, through the realization that "it's not about changing the world; it's about changing the square meter that
you're standing on."[35] Karen Elshazly adds that the experience of powerlessness that drives such perceptions need
not be urgent or dramatic; it can be a simple matter of dis-
covering one is a cog in a machine. "I've seen good people
just get burnt out on the UN bureaucracy," she says. "You
know, it's just so immovable and really so hard to accomplish the right things. Kind of like a good politician, who
enters with the enlightened view of changing the world
and then realizes that you have to really love to play the
games if you're going to make a difference."[36]

According to James Guy, this sort of internal contradiction between motive and capacity is typical, and the
cause of much of the burnout among aid workers. Guy is
the executive director and president of the Headington Institute, an organization based in Pasadena, California, that
offers psychological and spiritual counseling to humanitarian workers dealing with critical-incident stress, vicarious
trauma, and burnout. Until recently, many organizations
conceptualized their workers in terms that were very close
to a macho ethic, as people who didn't need or want help

(Kenneth Cain is of that unhelped generation of workers). But high burnout rates have increasingly come to be recognized as not only a psychological hazard for workers but also an *organizational* hazard with consequences for those receiving assistance. Staff turnover disrupts continuity of service, causes program delays, creates gaps in organizational memory, and drains financial resources (one study estimates the turnover cost for a manager at six months' salary or more)[37]—and all this, of course, is to say nothing of the unquantifiable effect that degenerating morale has on personal effectiveness in the field. Humanitarian organizations have, as a result, begun to change their practices. The Headington Institute is only six years old, about as old as the very idea of caring for the caregivers, and already it works with nearly a hundred organizations in more than fifty countries and has counseled well over a thousand workers.

In his time at the institute, James Guy has seen many people struggle in the same way Kenneth Cain has—it is a common thesis in psychology's burnout literature: "The more idealistic the individual is, the more vulnerable they are to being disappointed and then discouraged and then frustrated and burned out," Guy says. "With that being true, humanitarian workers as a group are among some of the most hopeful, idealistic, optimistic people around—initially, when they enter the field. You have to be, to want to do that kind of work." (I had to agree: almost uniformly among humanitarian workers I know, the response to the question "Why did you choose this work?" is embarrassing to them. They begin to say, sincerely, that they wanted to make a difference, that they wanted to help people—and then apologize for sounding trite and clichéd.) "So the very thing that brings them into the work," Guy sums up, "is something then that they have to struggle with, especially during those early years when they realize that the impact they can have is very limited, and most often is just only going to be about the individuals right in front of them."

Michael Ignatieff argues, similarly, that it is the very strength of our moral ambitions that makes us vulnerable to an immobilizing cynicism. "The gulf between what we've achieved and what we hope is continually growing, so we feel more and more hopeless. We don't have any excuses anymore. We have better information, better technology, and better resources than any time in history. And if you look at what those three things accomplish, they systematically pull out the excuses we have for leaving the world the way it is. That's why we feel more hopeless. It's because our capabilities have run far ahead of what we're now delivering." "I don't want my students to feel hopeless," he explained later, "just fantastically impatient."

Plato's story of the contradiction between desires, then, is in some ways emblematic of the perpetual ironies and incongruities of the humanitarian impulse: the motives that draw us in are often the hardest things for us to deal with. I spoke with Guy about the moral absolutists and idealists who enter a field requiring significant moral compromise, and about those who are able to achieve the confidence needed to enter the field largely because of what Guy calls their "grandiosity"—that is, their sense that love, their love, is special, and that it can change the world. When they realize it can't, that their personal sacrifices will never make the difference they desired—and they always learn this, early on—the despair can be as correspondingly profound as the hope, and can make continuing the work impossible. Some, moreover, find their love damaged: as Mary Anderson writes, some begin their missions "with genuine compassion and concern," only to end up developing a disillusioning "mistrust and disrespect" for those they have come to serve, largely because of the professionalized inequality of the giver-receiver relationship.[38] And as Mark Walkup explains, some aid workers experience the "limits of their effectiveness" as a kind of failure—a failure which begets guilt, which begets blame:

blame at the government, at the bureaucracy of their organization, even at the aid recipients themselves. He writes: "Refugees cease to be people *with* problems; refugees *become* the problem." Burnout, by such arguments, is altruism that surpasses our capacity to bear its strain.[39]

At the end of our conversation, Guy gave me one more example of the way our most powerful motivations can de-motivate us, hobble us. He says there is a subgroup among humanitarians, not commonly spoken of, "who have their own histories of being victims." He cited one study which revealed that the percentage of those recovering from physical and sexual abuse was notably higher among humanitarians than among the general population.

> One of the qualities we have as humans is that we seek to renew and redeem some of our own losses and pains. So some of the people that are drawn to the helping professions, and in particular to humanitarian work—they're kind of on a mission of recovery themselves. If they're far enough along that recovery, this is a great boost to it, because they can take what they've learned and sort of, by their own wounds and struggles, they can heal others. But for those that aren't that far along—you end up having rape victims who volunteer to interview refugees

who've been raped, and end up being retraumatized
by that work; or victims of violence who then
put themselves in humanitarian situations where they
could again become a victim of violence, or be vicari-
ously traumatized by being with victims of violence.

When I spoke with William Schulz, executive director
of Amnesty International USA, he listed some of the other,
less wrenching contradictions between the characteristics
likely to motivate people for such work and the characteristics needed to function well in an organization over time.
He affirmed that a strong sense of idealism and righteousness can be a crucial motivating trait for people seeking ca-
reers in human rights, but that it can also cause problems
in relationships with fellow workers and even with those
being helped. There is always the danger, he said, "that the
rescuer will somehow present him or herself as wiser than
the victim or in some way acting out a generosity that has
a double-edged nature to it." Moreover, he said, the sense
of "righteousness or self-righteousness" that some have
can translate into a tendency to become bitterly uncom-
promising in disagreements over strategies, priorities, or
resource allocation within an organization. Even the impulse for devotion and self-sacrifice, he added, can be an

impediment to organizational success. At Amnesty International and similar organizations, he said,

> we are trying to cast our small might on the side of life, and if we make a mistake . . . When you're dealing with such traumatic issues, such life-and-death issues, it feels like a lot is resting on your decisions—it may not in fact be [because you're simply not that powerful]—but it feels like a lot is resting on them. And if you're trying to get someone out of prison, or to stop them from being tortured, or especially to stop them from being executed, it feels as if: "Look, if we don't get our strategy right, if we don't organize assiduously enough, if we actually stop working at ten o'clock at night and go home and have a beer or whatever, if we don't devote as much of the twenty-four hours in a day as we physically can to this work, we're somehow failing people whose lives are in danger." And I think that's a tremendous risk, to fall into that trap. . . . What happens then is that people get exhausted, they get emotionally and physically exhausted, morally exhausted, they become angry at one another. I worked very hard with the staff . . . to get them to live balanced lives, and I tried to model

that myself, and to say that we really can't help other
people if we are completely drained and dissipated of
our own energies, resources, and wisdom.

Talking with Karen Elshazly about related staffing
challenges in humanitarian organizations, I mentioned the
T-shirt that figures in the novel *Cause Celeb*. She immediately identified this as a reference to what's known in the
field as the "3M theory": "mercenary, misfit, missionary."
Each brings its problems. As aid worker Matthew Bolton
writes, "The missionaries' earnestness can be a sustaining
factor but can be damaging when they impose their ideology onto a program of assistance. While the mercenary
types are often talented and pragmatic, it feels morally uncomfortable to see people exploiting human suffering for
material gain. Misfits think outside the box, but sometimes
an inferiority complex, or just plain weirdness, can get in
the way of a successful team."[40]

During my conversation with Elshazly, she focused on
mercenaries. "There are a few out there that are soldier-of-
fortune types," she said. "They kind of like the excitement
and like to be in danger zones, and you have to try and
weed them out because it can just really interfere with
how they do their work and how they respond to things."[41]
Some in this category, she noted, are attracted less to the

thrill than to the simple pleasures of the exotic and of
hierarchy:

> It's a constant diligence to make sure that we don't
> hire people that maybe are seeking a different life-
> style. You can be in some of these countries, and you
> can be a big fish in a little pond versus a little fish in
> a big pond, and that can go to your head if you're
> not prepared for that. . . . You can really get into
> some colonial-type feelings. . . . In most of these
> places, especially in Africa, because it's often insecure
> zones, we usually have communal housing for secu-
> rity and funding reasons, and they're out in the field
> all day. So of course there are house cleaners because
> it's too hard to do that on your own. But if I hear
> anyone use the word "servant"—believe me, I never
> talk to them again.

In rare cases, Elshazly noted, the mercenary devolves into
the baldly cynical. "I remember some of the food shipped
over to eastern Sudan in the Eighties—like cartons and cartons of chocolate wafers from ice cream sandwich bars. It's
a lot of dumping of things—medicines, for Western companies to get a tax write-off, when they might have ex-
pired." Even when the motivations aren't exploitive, she

notes, poorly planned resource dumping by mercenaries focused on the short term can have unintended negative consequences, like the creation of regional disparities. Her organization, by contrast, focuses on long-term capacity-building in troubled areas rather than only on short-term aid. "If you don't have an ongoing, reliable supply, it just doesn't help to have that one-time infusion. They're just a lot of crates of junk."

The disparities between motivation and effectiveness have their bitter parallel at the other end of the career arc: what makes the job rewarding and sustainable is also what makes it so difficult for workers to readjust to civilian life afterward—and readjustment (or "reentry," as it's often called) is inevitable, and typically occurs soon, because few people are able to maintain the physical stresses of fieldwork as they age. The average worker, Colleen Striegel claims, is a twenty- or thirty-something. Kenneth Cain believes those who stay in the field much past this age (instead of quitting altogether, or taking a desk job in headquarters as their primary position) are in some unconscious but deliberate fashion committing slow suicide.

For the young, however, such stresses are part of the addictive pleasure. "In the field," says Marco Jiménez Rodríguez, "you're moving from one adrenaline rush to the next, you're constantly challenged, you're speaking at least three languages every day, it is urgent every day. You wish for a normal life, but it can be hard to adjust to the pace of that life." Boredom, however, is merely the shadow of a larger existential problem. As James Guy puts it, thrill-addiction is part of the challenge of reentry. So, too, is the shock of abundance. But more profound is the question of what makes a meaningful life. The work, Guy says, "changes people at a pretty deep level. When you realize that so much of the world is struggling to survive, then how do you kind of gear down to a life that's much more routine, much less dramatic and urgent, without it starting to feel sort of petty and meaningless?" Many leave and come back, leave and come back, he said, "because they can't really find a place where they fit anymore." Brayne concurs: "Sitting quietly at home or having to fix the furnace or go to the children's sports day at school, when two days ago you were watching children die in Sudan—that's very, very hard. And it's extremely toxic for relationships and long-term emotional well-being." He adds that "working with clients in psychotherapy, the goal is to integrate their experience, to make meaning of it." It is, so to speak, a matter of constructing a coherent narrative, of taking "the pieces of the jigsaw" and getting "them all to fit together so that the individual can make sense of his or her life."

Kenneth Cain, as I've said, speaks openly about the difficulties of placelessness and reentry. But in some ways, for him, the deepest problem, the problem of meaning, has been partly resolved by the very crisis that caused his burnout. His life is filled with a sense of mission: namely, bringing about reform in the United Nations and in humanitarian work generally by exposing what he sees as their continual failures. Cain has a story to tell about the choices he made and he is, of late, extremely busy telling it, primarily because of the remarkable media controversy sparked in 2004, when officials at the United Nations attempted to stop publication of the book he wrote with Postlewait and Thomson. Internal UN regulations prohibit employees from publishing material without employer consent, and the UN did not consent. As Shashi Tharoor, the UN's under-secretary-general for communications and public information, told the *New Yorker:* "It didn't seem right for people to work for the organization and trash it the way these people did." Doing so while collecting a paycheck, he said, was "slightly contemptible."[42] (For its decision to resist—as should have been predictable—the United Nations was accused of book burning. Sales of the volume skyrocketed and it was optioned for television.)

But nobody that I met at the United Nations wanted to silence Cain, Thomson, and Postlewait. Most said they

were planning to read the book. In fact, I first heard about
the trio from Nancee Oku Bright, chief of the Advocacy
and Public Information Section at the UN's Office for the
Coordination of Humanitarian Affairs. I imagine that
when she finally reads the memoir, she'll find much to
sympathize with. It was clear to me from our interview
that she had no illusions about the UN's strengths or weak-
nesses, its successes or failures; indeed, she did not seem
like the kind of person to have illusions about any humanitarian organization's capacities (she strongly recom-
mended to me David Rieff's highly critical book *A Bed for
the Night*). "We fail people every day," she said, referring to
humanitarian efforts in general.

Nancee Oku Bright's willingness to frame problems in
institutional rather than personal terms reminded me of
something the organizational sociologist Charles Perrow
has said in different contexts: what we identify as the failing of an individual is often a system failure, a problem
that is built into the institution and that produces what he
calls "normal accidents."[43] Bright spoke to one structural
problem in particular, related to peacekeeping, and her
words resonated with Kenneth Cain's charges: "I think that
as a system we have to find out how to better train the
people who are there to serve and protect. I think that we
fail as a system when you send out—you know, you send

out soldiers, and you need to make sure that they understand what they're there to do, that they *are* soldiers. . . .
They're boys, they're eighteen, they're nineteen, they've
never seen battle in their lives, and then they see ten-year-
olds who are taking guns and who are taking machetes
and who are cutting people up and who are drugged. How
do you expect an eighteen-year-old or nineteen-year-old
from Uruguay to deal with some ten- or twelve-year-old
who actually has murdered people in ways you can't even
begin to envision?"

Bright had experienced many of the same frustrations
as Cain, and, like him, saw many things she cannot now
unsee. But like most everyone else I spoke to, she was
hesitant to use the word "trauma" for her emotional experiences—that word was reserved for the survivors. "I've
been through nothing—my God!" she said, surprised at
the suggestion. "I mean, people there are going through
it every day." Indeed, if anything, it is the many layers of
protection from actual trauma that are the most difficult
things for aid workers to live with emotionally. As Karen
Elshazly put it, describing the guilt that tinctures rescue:
"The hardest part is that you can drive away." Had this
work hurt Bright, then, in some other direct way? "I don't
know," she said. "If you're depressed, it's hard to say
whether your depression is linked to that or linked to

something else. I know that my boss, a very wonderful Swedish woman, told me that she thought I needed to go into therapy." I asked Bright what made her stay with this work, what made it rewarding. She started answering by telling a story—but the best way I can describe it, as strange as this sounds, is that the story started telling itself. Bright clearly hadn't talked to many people about what had happened; and as she tried to tell me a quick anecdote illustrating how the work had made her feel that she'd made a difference, she became increasingly sidetracked by vivid, detailed memories that pulled her further and further away from my question.

She'd been driving a van, under fire, around Bunya in the Congo, to collect wounded noncombatants and bring them back to her hospital for treatment. She met a man running a local clinic who asked if she could take some of his patients into her care. Space in the van was limited, so she asked the standard triage questions: How bad were the injuries? Could the patients walk to her facility if they had to? He quickly summarized the injuries, and said that the patients were doing okay and could walk. She told him she needed the space for more urgent cases but offered to drop him off at the clinic, since she would be passing that way to find a wounded man her group was looking for. When she got to the clinic, she decided to look in briefly, to

check on one of the women he had described. "I go in and
I find this woman who has to be all of four foot nothing,"
she said. "I mean she was tiny, she was skinny, she was in
her seventies. And they had chopped with a machete her
jaw, so her entire jaw was opened with her jawbone here
[Bright made a gesture]. They had chopped on the back of
the head, they had chopped off some of her fingers. This
was a little woman in her seventies. . . . What do you have
to fear from somebody like that? She's past her childbear-
ing years, there's nothing that she can do to harm you."
The mutilation was extensive, but it was neither the injuries nor the woman's age that really shook Bright. It was,
rather, how banal they had sounded when described from
the perspective of the clinic operator.

There was another woman, in a river of blood, Bright
recalled, continuing the story. The killers had chopped
her across the abdomen and then rammed the machete
through her vagina. She would not live. Bright loaded the
elderly woman with the damaged jaw into the van, and
they continued their search. When they finally reached the
wounded man they were looking for, he was alive but
clearly failing. When they got him back to the UN hospital, they turned him over to an Italian doctor. The doctor
approached him and slid his hands under his shirt to peel
it off. When he did so, the pants came apart suddenly as

well. "And there are maggots everywhere. The guy's entire lower body is being consumed by maggots. The Italian doctor—I'm sure he'd never seen anything like this before—he jumps back. This guy is just lying there. All here, all here," she gestured to her stomach, groin, and upper thighs. "This is a black man completely covered in white. Maggots everywhere. They're just eating him up." She paused. "He survived for a few days, but there was no way really to save this guy. Although the doctor said it was the maggots that were actually fighting the bacteria. But he died." She paused again. "Other people didn't die," she continued, inflecting her tone upward and returning finally to my original question. "I think that was probably the best part of my experience." She stopped suddenly and turned her back to me for a while, collecting herself. "The best and the worst were definitely the same."

When Nancee Oku Bright had entered the profession, she had done so with a different sort of idealism from Kenneth Cain's; and because of this she had been able to return, bearing many of the same troubles, and continue her efforts (she plans to leave headquarters regularly to work in the field). Time and time again when we spoke, Bright continually figured her hope in terms of others: the possibilities of the next generation, what those who come after us might be able to do. "These kids now—who's to say if they're not the ones who will make a difference?" She held her hope at a distance; she had hope for the hope of others. It seemed to me that it was much safer that way.

██████ I would like to close this consideration of what might be called the psychology of humanitarianism with two comments on hope. The first is by Noam Chomsky, from a conversation we had about hope and activism shortly before I began this project. Hope is something like Pascal's Wager, he said. "You have two choices. You can say there's no hope, I'm not going to bother—in which case you guarantee that the worst will happen. Or you can say, 'Look, realistically, there's a chance that things will get better, therefore I'll become involved in it, and then maybe the worst won't happen—in fact, maybe something good will happen.' Those are basically the choices. Where you find yourself in the spectrum of hopefulness is a personal matter of no significance. The choices are the same no matter where you find yourself."

I remembered these words when I asked James Guy the same question about hope, and he replied by telling me an oft-repeated anecdote about Mother Teresa. As different as the two responses were, they both captured, it seemed to me, a quality common to many of the more experienced humanitarian workers I knew—a quality simultaneously gentle and stubborn, kind and distant. In Guy's version of the story, Mother Teresa was walking through the streets of Calcutta, "being followed by a newspaper reporter. And after about half a day of just following her, watching her minister to one person at a time on the streets—holding their hands, giving them a hug, offering them some food, or praying with them—he finally said to her, 'How do you ever expect that, with all of these people in need, you're making any difference at all? How do you expect to be successful?' And she paused and she said, 'You know, it never occurred to me to be successful. I'm just trying to be obedient.'"

4 STORYTELLING

I

A number of the human rights advocates and humanitarian workers we've met thus far are also artists, or found themselves turning to art as a way of working through their experiences, whether in the form of film (Nancee Oku Bright, Rony Brauman), memoir (Roméo Dallaire, Clea Koff, Kenneth Cain), or, as we'll see in this chapter, novels. John Coyne, a former Peace Corps volunteer in Ethiopia, claims that "three hundred and fifty returned Peace Corps Volunteers have published books, many of which have been based on their experiences overseas."[1] The kinship between professional storytelling and humanitarian work is especially close in the world of journalism. Donatella Lorch is well known as a war correspondent and writer for the *New York Times, Newsweek,* and NBC, but she began her career as a relief worker in the refugee camps of

Pakistan. She told me about a colleague of hers from National Public Radio who, after covering the heart-sickening story of the refugee camps in Goma, asked to be released for a period of leave—which he then spent as a volunteer in one of the feeding centers, because, as Lorch put it, "he needed to feel that he was making a difference, that he was helping."

This chapter is about the photography, journalism, theater, and literature of human rights. Earlier chapters examined storytelling as an instrument of human rights work, from rescuing survivors to sustaining the psychic well-being of fieldworkers. Here we will look at human rights storytelling that has a different goal—or, rather, that is its own goal. As writer and journalist David Rieff told me:

> Aid workers tell stories for all kinds of reasons. They tell stories to try to get attention to some crisis that they feel needs remedy. The ones who are more involved in human rights issues will tell stories to denounce some bad behavior somewhere, some crime or grave breach, or to try to motivate an intervention, military intervention or political intervention. And then lastly and somewhat more ambiguously they do it to publicize their own organization's work. So they have rather more concrete goals. Telling the

story is a vehicle for continuing a specific kind of
work they're doing. For me telling the story or making an analysis is an end in itself.

Rieff's comment was typical of many (not all, but
many) of the writers and visual artists I spoke with. Gov-
erned by a sense that they couldn't make a difference in
the world—or at least any predictable difference, any kind
of difference they could see or control—many said the
same thing when asked what they were hoping to achieve
with their words and pictures. In almost identical words,
each time, they told me they just wanted *to say something
that was true.* Their hopes, and what they saw as their responsibility, extended no further than that.

But the problems involved in saying something true are
in some ways just as intractable as the problems involved
in all the humanitarian interventions this book has considered. As one early reader of this manuscript said: "Who
nominates you to publicize pain and suffering that you
can walk away from? How does one avoid the trap of
commodifying intense suffering to elicit maximum effect
(or career advantage)?" How do you resolve the paradox
that your audiences hunger for these images and stories
of calamity both because they want to understand their
world and their moral responsibilities in it, and because
they are narrowly voyeuristic?

Perhaps the best way to start answering these questions is with the story of one the most highly visible untaken photographs of the past several decades. During Bangladesh's war of independence from Pakistan, in 1971, Bengali soldiers paraded a group of Bihari prisoners before an angry crowd at the Dhaka racetrack. It was a tense, volatile scene. There were several photographers present, including Marc Riboud. Riboud was no stranger to violence. He had fought in the French Resistance during the 1940s and had been invited by Henri Cartier-Bresson and Robert Capa to join Magnum Photos, a group established after World War II that, as one founding member explained, had come into itself "during several years of contact with all the emotional excesses that go hand in hand with war."[2]

Here's how Riboud described the spectacle at Dhaka when we talked:

> At the end of this meeting the Bengalese, they had assembled about six or eight boys, guys, they were held together with ropes on their hands. . . . They could not move; they were alive. . . . The militia of the new regime started to torture them in the most terrible way. There was a group—I could not—when I saw blood starting I did not even stop and take pictures. At the beginning they were beating them, but they started to put incredible—I couldn't describe. I

saw blood coming out of the eyes and the nose. And there was one guy, probably the brother of one of those who were there, who was crying, praying, praying with his two hands those torturers to stop. And after a while, of course, a torturer took this guy and put him in the circle with the others. And he was put slowly to death by torture. But before—I could not stand, I did not take pictures—there were three other European photographers [who took pictures]. I knew them. When I had seen that, I was sick.

Riboud tried in a panic to find some Indian officers, desperate to make the killers stop, but the crowd was too chaotic and he couldn't find any. Later, far away, when it was all over, Riboud met with two of the photographers who had remained behind to shoot the scene. They described how the violence and degradation had escalated, how the prisoners had been killed, how people had urinated on their corpses. "I could not photograph such a scene behind the torturers, taking no risk," Riboud said.

According to Harold Evans, former editor of the *Times* of London, Riboud was among a group at the scene who, watching how things developed, "felt that their cameras were inciting the soldiers."[3] The photographs were awarded the Pulitzer Prize. Evans declared the decision "demeaning to photojournalism."[4] John Morris, picture editor at the *New York Times* when the editors decided to run one of the photos on the front page, called the prize well deserved and described the photographs as "a public service."[5]

When I asked Riboud thirty-five years later if he indeed thought things happened the way they did because the soldiers were playing to the cameras—if, in other words, the cameras were complicit in what happened—he hesitated, because he was very reluctant to put any blame on the other photographers. His own attempt to intervene, he admitted with shame, was feeble. He didn't expect the others to stand in front of the bayonets. What else could they do but shoot the pictures? "It's not that I refused to photograph," Riboud said. "I just *couldn't*." One of the photographers, Michel Laurent, was killed four years later covering the defense of Saigon, as he attempted to help a wounded man. "Those limits," Riboud said, "nobody can draw them. I never blamed those photographers." In the end, however, he said he believes that at Dhaka "the torturers were doing it to be seen, to be photographed." It was a performance. "They wanted to show their hatred, their anger, against the occupied enemy by showing they are able to kill the enemy." They wanted "humiliation."

Riboud told me that immediately afterward he flew to

Delhi and put in a request for an audience with Prime Minister Indira Gandhi. Gandhi invited him to meet her at her home. They greeted each other and then sat quietly for some time, looking at each other. Something had to be said, to be done, but Riboud did not know how to start, what to say. "I could not even tell the story of the blood of what I saw." But Gandhi already knew. She, like everyone else in the world, had seen what had happened, because of the pictures that had been taken. When they finally began to speak, Gandhi made it clear to Riboud that the publication of these pictures had made the massacre into a worldwide shame, and that "the reputation of India was at stake." Something would be done.

And so, Riboud said, "about the photographers, I went through different feelings. I had to agree that the photographs taken became very useful to stop this." And perhaps it didn't even matter why they shot the pictures, even if "the photographers did it without much thinking, because they were amazed, because they were in front of an incredible event." What matters is that the pictures were taken. The people caught up in that conflict were better off—it might be argued that we are *all* collectively better off—because there are people who are willing to take such pictures.

Photojournalist Ron Haviv remembers witnessing the

execution of two people in 1991, during the war in Croatia. It happened so fast he didn't have time to think about it. "As I lifted my camera up," he told me, "I had guns put to my head." From that moment on, he resolved that "if there was nothing I could do to actually stop an execution, the least I wanted to do was be able to walk away with evidence." Haviv has suffered consequences for his work—he has been threatened, detained, beaten, and subjected to mock executions—but he has taken the pictures because he believes it's important.[6] His photographs have been used as evidence at the International Criminal Tribunal for the Former Yugoslavia. Another war photographer put it this way when we spoke about Dhaka: Yes, maybe people were executed there because cameras were present. But how many people have *not* been executed elsewhere because cameras were present?

This is a compelling question. But even in cases when complicity or endangerment is not an issue—when the cameras are by no reasonable standards implicated in the injuries, when in fact it is widely hoped that they will directly or indirectly save lives—even then the moral strain of the work remains. Susan Sontag describes an especially painful example of the work's difficulty, of the way its hopes couple with revulsion: "In Sarajevo in the years of the siege, it was not uncommon to hear, in the middle of a bombardment or burst of sniper fire, a Sarajevan yelling at the photojournalists, who were easily recognizable by the equipment hanging round their necks, 'Are you waiting for a shell to go off so you can photograph some corpses?' . . . [And yet] most of the many experienced journalists who reported from Sarajevo were not neutral. And the Sarajevans did want their plight to be recorded in photographs: victims are interested in the representation of their own sufferings."[7]

Sontag's son, David Rieff, covered the siege of Sarajevo as a writer. "There are all kinds of moral problems with reporting, most obviously being voyeurism," he told me. "It's most evident in photojournalism, because you're looking for a shot of something that is arresting. In Sarajevo, the Sarajevans used to think that the journalists went to street corners where snipers were particularly lethal, and they sometimes called the photographers the 'angels of death.' I think print reporters like myself are equally guilty—it's just not as obvious." One war correspondent described it to me as the problem of "enabling the voyeurism of others." "The misery of Bosnia," journalist Peter Maass writes, "sold well in the summer and fall of 1992"—but interest gradually died off, because "even snuff films get boring after a while."[8]

Yet when I discussed the issue with Donatella Lorch, she

said she was troubled less by what people are able to see because of war reporting and photography than by what they are unable to see. She referenced pictures of casualties in Iraq from an American bombing: "The one in particular that comes to mind is that little girl being pulled out of a bombed house, I think in Basra, where one of her legs has just been blown away and you can see the bone sticking out. That picture ran in the United States with the leg cropped out." That was wrong, she said. "The reality of war is ugly, and we shouldn't be able to look away."

The controversial images of the killings at Dhaka, the siege of Sarajevo, and the war in Iraq raise many questions about the representation of atrocity, about the way we have made an industry of images of atrocity. What are we obliged to reveal, and what to veil? What does it mean to reward such acts of witnessing? When does nonintervention amount to complicity? How much can your specialized role as a chronicler immunize you from your moral responsibilities as a human? Is the work a matter of moral luck? That is, if your work ends up making a positive difference you are a servant of the public good, but if it is ignored you are merely a voyeur, a pornographer of pain? Or do personal motives trump consequences (and if so, what degree of "mixed motives" can we tolerate)? What are the structural, built-in moral problems of this sort of work, and how can we try to minimize the damage they may cause?

Ron Haviv portrays the difficulties in photojournalism as a matter of the queasy gap between short-term and long-term moral value. He told me about his work documenting the monstrous Serbian paramilitary leader Arkan (Željko Ražnatović), "who was responsible for killing thousands of people. There was no way for me even to have been with them [Arkan's Tigers] had he not sort of trusted me and thought that I was on his side. It's even something as basic as, you know, agreeing with his political viewpoints. You have to befriend these murderers in order to gain access to them." Together with this discomfort, Haviv described something seemingly a world away: the publicity work of exhibitions. "On the opening night, nobody's really looking at the work and everybody's drinking and celebrating while these photographs of atrocity are on the wall." The "opening-night situation," he said, "it's so vulgar." But "the more people that come to see the work and talk about the work—in the end, that's what you're trying to achieve, and that's to the greater good."

The ethical problems of representing violence for the public are perhaps most dramatic in photography; but as Rieff suggests, they are no less painful in print journalism, nonfiction, and even fiction. Michael Montgomery is a for-

mer correspondent for the *Daily Telegraph* and producer at
CBS News who now produces public-radio documentaries.
For him, as for Riboud, the key ethical difficulties of the
work lie not in your relationship with your audience, but
in the relationship you establish with the people in front of
you, the ones whose stories you will tell. "We have this
idea that the simple act of bearing witness is what matters
to survivors, but it's far more complicated than that. When
you come and interview them, their hope is that their lives
are going to improve, that they're going to be helped by
this in some tangible way. So they tell you their stories,
these painful stories, and you listen knowing that you're almost certainly not going to help them. It's not deception,
but sometimes it comes close to feeling like it."

Worse, Montgomery notes, even the promise to bear
witness that is implicit in the interview process—the mere
promise to listen and to tell the story without any idea
that this might help—even this promise must often be broken. He recalls a story he did in Rwanda where he and a
female colleague "pushed" to get interviews from a group
of women who'd been raped during the genocide and in-
fected with the HIV virus. "When it was all done, we felt
that what we got out of the interview was not worth what
we put these women through. And you know what? Most
of their stories didn't even make it into the piece."

Dave Eggers, who recently launched an oral-history series on human rights crises, "Voice of Witness," through
his independent press McSweeney's, expanded on Montgomery's concerns when we talked:

> One of the things that journalists and human rights
> workers who take these accounts might be feeling is
> that feeling that they've emotionally drained some-
> body or retraumatized them, and then left. And in
> many cases they've left the person with nothing, and
> the person has nothing to show for it. They don't
> have anything physically in their hands: like, well,
> here's a transcript of what I've said, now I know that
> the UNHCR has heard my story. They don't know
> that. They don't really know who that person is, they
> don't know what's come of it. All the people that
> I've met over the years, when I've finished an in-
> terview, that's all they want: Well, what's going to
> happen now? What are you going to do? Who are
> you going to tell? Are you going to send help? You
> know, that's what they want. And I think without
> leaving them with anything tangible, we as inter-
> viewers can get a sense that we've stolen something.
> That aspect of theft that we can feel as journalists or
> human rights documentarians. Like: I came in, I stole

something from you, I *took* your story, and you'll
never see me again. That's what I think human rights
workers and interviewers sometimes feel, is that there
isn't an ongoing relationship, it's just a theft and that's
it, and the position of power that they have. They can
go back to Amsterdam or New York or wherever, and
take that story and publish it, and pat themselves on
the back for having gotten it. But the person that they
took it from has in many cases gotten nothing.

John Matthews (not his real name) is a journalist who
works for a prominent national publication. When I asked
him about the moral difficulties of his work, he described
a story he once ran about a Marine who died in Iraq (I will
not reveal any details here, out of consideration for the soldier's family). The story he'd published was painful, the details agonizing to read—but they were important to share
with the public, he believed. It was, he said, "just one of
the horrible ways death can happen during a war . . . a reminder of the death that happens during war, and the
cost of war." After he ran the story, he discovered that the
soldier's family had only been "given the scantest of information by the Marines" about how he'd died. They had
learned very difficult things about their son's final moments by reading a magazine article.

But Matthews felt, and still feels, that he did the right thing in telling the story, that his role required it:

> It is somewhat standard actually that the US military, and every military for that matter, gives out very little information to families about the causes of death for their loved ones. And sometimes the military gives out erroneous information, too; think of the whole controversy about Pat Tillman—you know, the former professional football player who was killed in Afghanistan. You know the Army basically lied about what happened. He was killed by friendly fire, but the Army, for its own propaganda purposes and to avoid embarrassment, tried to portray it as being a fierce gun battle in which he was fighting against Al-Qaeda. So there's a very good purpose served by journalists writing about how Marines and soldiers actually do die in combat. And it can be uncomfortable for family members to read. But it's not all family members who necessarily are made uncomfortable; and what's making them uncomfortable—the root of it, in a way—is, at least from my perspective, that they're not being told by the military and that they have to read about it in a magazine. That's the problem. So, yes, it is very hard to be

the bearer of that news about how somebody died,
but it's something that needs to be done.

Even believing this, however, Matthews didn't publish
the full story about the Marine's death. Here's what he
never told: he had reason to believe that the soldier could
have been saved. By one account, fellow Marines nearby
must have heard his cries for help, but they hadn't ventured
out into the dark that night to give assistance, because they
were afraid it was an Iraqi trap. "Given the costs involved
in reporting it," he said, "in terms of the anguish that I
thought it might cause for the family of the Marine who'd
died, I thought: Just put this one aside . . . It was mainly for
the family. My instinct at the time was that this family has
enough to deal with, [without having] this second thought
for the rest of their lives. . . . Then you get into questions
of, you know, my God, he could've been saved."

Antjie Krog's *Country of My Skull* and Gillian Slovo's
Red Dust are especially painful examples of the way such
paradoxes of private trauma and public duty can arise in
nonfiction books and even novels. They are both accounts
of South Africa's Truth and Reconciliation Commission
(TRC), arguably one of the most important acts of collective storytelling in the history of human rights work. The
TRC was also, it should be noted, extremely self-conscious

about the moral risks and imperatives of its own story-telling. On the one hand, the TRC in its final report was overwhelmingly positive in its self-evaluation, describing frequently the "therapeutic process" of "giving survivors an opportunity to tell their stories," and the "healing po-tential of telling stories."[9] It even described how survi-vors approached the Commission "in an almost foetal po-sition," but after telling their stories "walked tall."[10] On the other hand, the Commission also publicly acknowl-edged the moral complexities of its work and its hurtful failures, including the criticism of Thenjiwe Mtintso, dep-uty secretary general of the African National Congress, who attacked the TRC's program of therapy: "Some of the women whose wounds you opened—we did not pay enough time or give them enough opportunity to heal once they left these halls. I have been to Cape Town, where there were hearings, Chairperson. I have been to Port Elizabeth. I have been to King William's Town. There are wounds that have been left gaping. . . . You cannot open them in this hall and leave them gaping. Somebody has got to take responsibility."[11]

Eric Stover, director of the Human Rights Center at the University of California, Berkeley, spent several years inter-viewing survivors who gave testimony at the Rwanda and Yugoslavia Tribunals (institutions that are very different from the TRC, it should be emphasized, but relevant nonetheless as instances of the risks entailed in collecting survivor testimony). Stover was very critical of human rights advocates and lawyers who "use this language of how justice is catharsis, justice will right the world." As he put it:

> Of course we need to have justice, but it's very, very difficult for the victims to go through this process of testifying. . . . Of the eighty-seven that I interviewed, a few of them [twelve, according to his book *The Witnesses*][12] had catharsis when they came out of the trial. Others were devastated under cross-examination. They were so confident when they went into the trial, and they were devastated because the defense brought up something that just threw them off. And then they walk out, the prosecutor isn't there to tell them they've done a good job, they're a stranger in a strange land, and they're flown home. They go home and they then are faced with walking back into their bombed-out apartment or dealing with a life where they have no job or their kid can't go to a good school, and so on. . . . Anybody who romanticizes this, in my view, has it dead, dead wrong.

Gillian Slovo's *Red Dust* is a fictional account of the TRC, but, as with so much fiction, its invented characters and plot lines are at least in part composites of real people and events. The novel, like the TRC itself, is self-conscious about the deep moral problems of its own storytelling. Indeed, it takes as a central concern the moral problems entailed in the storytelling of all human rights work, exploring some of the very same issues of humanitarian inquisition we examined earlier with regard to the work of the UNHCR. In *Red Dust*, a lawyer working in New York has returned to her home in South Africa to represent a torture survivor, Alex Mpondo, who must face his torturer at an amnesty hearing. The lawyer learns that even the work of justice, perhaps *especially* the work of justice, can be psychically crushing for those it is meant to vindicate. Her efforts to prepare for the hearing, for instance, involve asking Mpondo questions, pressing for answers, checking discrepancies—interrogating him, essentially, in a way that outrages his friends, who see it as a "crucifixion" evocative of his original torture.[13]

The rueful hearings that Slovo depicts after this ominous beginning are in part based upon the notorious amnesty hearings of police captain Jeffrey Benzien. Antjie Krog, who covered the hearings as a radio broadcaster, describes in her own nonfiction book *Country of My Skull* how Benzien, when confronted by his victims face-to-face at the TRC, managed to manipulate "most of his victims back into the roles of their previous relationship—where he has the power and they the fragility." Writing of one torture survivor who is surely a partial source for Slovo's Mpondo, Krog concludes that for his moment of public acknowledgment, he "has to pay dearly." The torturer is exposed, but so is the tortured: "Do you remember, Mr. Yengeni," Benzien says to the court, "that within thirty minutes you betrayed Jennifer Schreiner? Do you remember pointing out Bongani Jonas to us on the highway?"[14]

"I want it to end," *Red Dust's* Mpondo says of the hearings in anticipation of such exposure. "I want it to end."[15]

But it does not. In a painful turn of the screw, Krog's exposure of the TRC's structural cruelty—the way the Commission caused some survivors to relive their original traumatic helplessness—became, itself, a doubling of this repetition (and has yet again, since it was made into a clumsy film by Sony Pictures Classics). As Kay Schaffer and Sidonie Smith write of survivors' responses to Krog's book: "Some recoiled from her profiling of their pain; others failed to recognize themselves through the perceptions of the writer; still others resented what seemed to them as an appropriation of their pain to her project of reconciliation."[16]

Krog—like all those confronting the paradox that trauma is fundamentally unsharable yet *must* be shared if change is to occur—wrote with her heart in her throat.

"That is why I say maybe writers in South Africa should shut up for a while," she says tentatively about literature after apartheid. "That one has no right to appropriate a story paid for with a lifetime of pain and destruction."[17] As Thandi Shezi, a survivor of torture and rape under apartheid, is reported to have said of her appearance at the TRC: "It feels like I was abused all over again. With the TRC, it felt like all they wanted was my story. I felt used." And yet, as the final twist in this cruel moral paradox, the survivors of such atrocities also often want their stories to be shared. Despite the trauma, concludes Shezi, "going to the TRC was a victory. . . . It gave me a platform to share my grief. It made me talk. Hopefully, I will heal in time."[18]

Compared with the works of Krog and Slovo, Ping Chong's *Children of War*—part of his series of oral-history theater pieces collectively titled *Undesirable Elements*—occupies an even more difficult space between reportage and art, performance and testimony. Chong recruited children who had come to the United States as war refugees, interviewed them about some of the most painful details of their traumatic personal histories, and then turned those interviews into a theatrical production performed by the children themselves.

FATU: We hear SCREAMING in the market. Everybody runs.

FARINAZ: "Do you want a short sleeve or a long sleeve?"

FATU: THAT *is what the boy killers ask.*

   AWA: If you say long sleeve they chop off your entire arm.

YARVIN: If you say short sleeve, they chop off your arm at the elbow.

   FATU: People run past me screaming, with no arms.

     ALL CLAP.[19]

When I first heard about the project, I was troubled. I was troubled by the risk for the children, and the possibility that their audiences might be composed of voyeurists of terror or bored, purposeless people seeking an "authentic" moment. After talking to Chong and reading accounts of the reactions of the children, however, I was persuaded that this was a powerfully therapeutic and affirming experience for the children and communities involved.[20] Chong was highly sensitive to the risks of the work, and collaborated with counselors and social workers from the Center for Multicultural Human Services in northern Virginia. The children were eager to tell their stories, having spent much of their time in the United States feeling that nobody could understand or even believe them. They were participants in creating something almost tangible rather than subjects of a large process. It seemed to me that this feeling of control, together with the relationships of mutual vulnerability they developed, could perhaps make all the difference.

Farinaz Amirsehi was the only adult to perform with

the children. She had been imprisoned in Iran for more than seven years for speaking out against the regime of the Ayatollah Khomeini (she was released early because of the advocacy of Amnesty International). When we spoke, she recalled the small acts of control, and in particular of aesthetic expression, that had helped her to survive her detention and torture. When she was blindfolded and confined in a small space they called "the graves," she designed a hospital in her head, down to the number of meters of piping it would require; walking the pathway to her interrogations, she collected pebbles which she would later carve with a bobby pin; forced to listen to readings of the Koran twenty-four hours a day, she reimagined the passages as operas in foreign languages.

They controlled everything in prison, she explained: "Your language, your whole body language, you name it, I mean the thoughts that you have, the dreams that you want to have." They controlled you in the worst ways. "You're afraid that you're going to break down; you know it's coming. The guilt of it just kills you, anticipating the guilt just kills you. What if I can't take it anymore and I give out names? This was the worst part. I would rather be executed ten thousand times."

In its own small way, Farinaz said, the process of creating the play was an inversion of these self-erasing experiences. "You had control over things, what to say, what not to say. Ping was wonderful, he would work with you. If you didn't want to talk about this part—okay, that was out, even though it was a very interesting part. He never pressured anyone on their stories. . . . It was empowering because it was the first time for most of us to tell our story thoroughly, the way we wanted to say it, as much as we wanted to say it, and to still be received." With the *Children of War* project, she said, "we had become a family. It was safe there."

II

In all the cases discussed in the previous section, if there was any moral anxiety it derived from the fact that there were real bodies behind the words, specific people who could feel exposed, ashamed, exploited. In the most extreme case, at Dhaka, there were real people who could be physically endangered. Riboud's choices there might mark the extreme end of the ethical spectrum facing those who make stories out of violence, but, as other cases reveal, such choices are not as rare as we might imagine.

Haviv described the situation to me as a "constant ethical dilemma." Photographers, he said, need "to understand when people around them are doing something for the benefit of the camera. There's been a number of times where I've seen soldiers acting up because they knew there was a camera there, or offering to shoot people or do something just for the benefit of the camera. It's a very important line not to cross."[21]

Peter Maass recalls being allowed into Omarska (a detention facility in northern Bosnia) by Serbian authorities intent on repudiating claims that it was a torture center; journalists like Maass entered intent on proving that it was. He saw a television crew filming a sick prisoner in his bed, asking him in front of the guards if he was being treated well. "Obviously he could not speak honestly," Maass writes, "but the guard might get mad if he was too fulsome in his praise. The truth would kill, and even the wrong lie would kill. . . . It was a sort of Russian roulette. Five empty chambers in the gun, one filled with a bullet. The reporter was handing the gun to the prisoner when he turned the camera on. *Speak,* the reporter asked. *Pull the trigger.*" When Maass approached prisoners in what he felt was a more discreet and professionally appropriate way, one begged him in a whisper, "Please, don't ask me questions."[22] Jeri Laber raises much the same issue in her memoir of her years as a journalist and as a founding member of Helsinki Watch: telling the stories of her meetings with dissidents—indeed, simply meeting with dissidents to hear their stories—could endanger their lives.[23]

Choosing to represent people or, rather, to make them into a representation, can in many circumstances function like coercion, threat, and violence. But this is, admittedly, the extreme end of the spectrum. The accounts by Michael Montgomery and the war correspondent working in Iraq reveal that the more representative ethical dilemmas for writers occur at a significant distance from immediate and brute physical endangerment. The injuries people suffer in these cases are no less real, but they are less physical. In the case of *Red Dust,* we are pulled even further away from Dhaka and Omarska, further and further up the ethical spectrum toward increasingly imagined worlds and increasingly indirect possibilities of harm. But even here, what feels potentially troubling is that real people served as material for the novel, and that real people could in perhaps damaging ways recognize themselves in its details.

In what follows I would like to move further along the spectrum than even *Red Dust* took us. I would like to talk about human rights and the moral problem of purely fictional worlds. More precisely, I want to talk about the ethics of representation in artworks when they are, rightly or wrongly, *experienced* as purely fictional worlds, when the primary concern is not the safety or dignity of persons but, rather, the dignity of aesthetic enterprise and the morality of form itself.

This final section, then, is about the aesthetic forms
that have blossomed alongside the towering (to some, im-
posing, imperializing) concept of universal human rights.
It is about the fictional worlds that have developed together with, and as a way of thinking about, our all-too-
real political worlds. Emerging with global human rights
culture—or, as this book has tried to show, alongside the
many cultures of human rights around the globe—is an astonishing body of fictional literature, from Iran to the
United States, South Africa to Argentina, Sri Lanka to the
Dominican Republic, with common aesthetic properties
and thematic concerns. Human rights stories, it might even
be proposed, have begun to coalesce as a self-contained set
of texts sharing key formal properties, an emerging global
subgenre that can help to structure high-school and college
teaching and research, and that can illuminate urgent questions about the relationships among representation,
beauty, ethics, and politics.[24]

In what follows I will take only provisional steps toward making this particular genre-argument, and will do
so primarily as a way of organizing discussion of the cen-
trifugal questions it raises about the representation of atrocity. A full examination of the features and coherence of
the "novel of human rights" is material for another book.
Here I will consider only a very small cluster of such

works, focusing on the most widely known authors of human rights fiction (J. M. Coetzee, Michael Ondaatje, Dave Eggers) together with a small but, I believe, representative cluster of novelists I've talked with who have significant experience in human rights and humanitarian work—novelists who were in some sense compelled to write their stories because of the experiences they had. Included among these writers are Alan Cumyn, author of the torture novels *Man of Bone* and *Burridge Unbound,* who worked for many years at the Immigration and Refugee Board of Canada researching human rights; Farnoosh Moshiri, author of the prison novels *The Bathhouse* and *At the Wall of the Almighty,* who was a feminist and activist in Iran before fleeing under threat of death; Lawrence Thornton, author of *Imagining Argentina* (now a major film) and two sequels about the Dirty War, who was an antiwar activist; Douglas Unger, author of a novel about the disappeared, *Voices from Silence,* who in the 1980s was involved in researching Argentina's disappearances and who currently is on the advisory board of the Cities of Asylum Network; and Annechristine d'Adesky, author of *Under the Bone,* a novel about human rights during the regimes of Haitian dictators François and Jean-Claude Duvalier. D'Adesky was a human rights reporter in Haiti for many years and is now an AIDS activist, having established a clinic in Rwanda that treats HIV-positive women. Gillian Slovo's *Red Dust* likewise developed out of the intense pressures of personal experience. Slovo told me that her distressing experience at South Africa's Truth and Reconciliation Commission—confronting the men complicit in the assassination of her mother, a radical anti-apartheid activist in the 1960s and 1970s—compelled her to abandon her original plans for a tightly plotted story about the TRC and to create instead a complex and emotionally ambivalent novel.

I would like to begin this look at the fictions of human rights generally by returning to the TRC and Slovo's novel. When prospective commissioners for the TRC were being interviewed in public hearings, one candidate rejected the possibility of reconciliation: "This Truth Commission thing is useless," he declared. "Only literature can perform the miracle of reconciliation."[25] Slovo rejects this romanticized vision of literary art both as possibility and responsibility, and rejects it in a way that is representative of much fiction about atrocity. At first glance, however, *Red Dust* does indeed seem structured as a narrative of reconciliation and closure. It tracks the successful revelation of apartheid's abuses through the work of the TRC and concludes when a long-suffering father finally recovers his son's body for burial and murders the supervisor of his boy's unspeakable torture. But the novel is incapable of ending without undermining the satisfaction this rough justice delivers. In a perverse twist, the father is spared prosecution for murder by the lies of the wife of the man he murdered. She provides him an alibi, but apparently only so that she can maintain some form of structural control over this formerly subservient black man, and so that she can defy what the TRC has attempted to achieve in South Africa by forcing him to live a lie, to carry the past like a shameful secret. The torture survivor Alex Mpondo makes a telling observation about an activist lawyer in the novel—a woman who, like many idealistic Westerners, yearns for miracles: she had "forgotten that the story with a beginning, a middle and its own neat ending, which was what she'd tried to give him, was something New York might offer, but not South Africa. There was too much history here, too much bad history, for that kind of completion."[26]

The most basic narrative pull of so many of the novels that take human rights violations as their central plot concern, from Michael Ondaatje's *Anil's Ghost* to J. M. Coetzee's *Waiting for the Barbarians,* is hope. What draws readers through the landscapes of ruined bodies is the hope of a just conclusion. But even as each novel works hard to maintain reader interest with that tantalizing promise of recompense, each is also deeply skeptical about the satisfaction that any justice can deliver. As a case study in what rights-oriented authors like Slovo and others seek to avoid, take Kathy Reichs's pulp thriller *Grave Secrets*. Here, the human rights plot with which the novel begins (recovering the remains of villagers massacred at Chupan Ya in Guatemala) is more or less discarded as the Chupan Ya excavation lures the protagonist into the web of a more traditional detective story, complete with murdered social-ites and an international "dirty cell-harvesting scheme." Like Marcus Wynne in his torture-thriller *Brothers in Arms* (which features a much distorted Center for Victims of Torture), Reichs uses a quick-and-easy human rights setup to gild her book with moral purpose and elevate it within the genre. By the end, the gratifying success in unraveling the (non–human rights) murder mysteries blends happily into the recovery work at Chupan Ya, to which the novel returns briefly with trivializing, contented closure: the bod-ies are recovered, the village experiences "an enormous sense of relief," and the rights workers enjoy "the feeling of a tough job well-done."[27]

Many authors who deal seriously with the representa-tion of human rights violations are suspicious of such "de-tective novel" tendencies.[28] Such narrative closure, along with the ethical closure it entails, leaves us comfortable rather than unsettled; it delivers an energy-releasing catharsis, a feeling that the world is indeed just and that such atrocities do not require our continued moral fury. Justice suggests clarity, completion, and proportion: x has been compensated by y. But the point of much of this literature is that we are caught in a terrible double-bind: we must seek recompense even though we know there can never be any recompense.[29] And we must produce novels readers will wish to read, novels that deliver some form of narrative closure and satisfaction, even while recounting histories defined by *lack* of closure (the 1982 Guatemalan massacres that Reichs uses as material, for instance, were part of a thirty-six-year civil war which, though officially over by 1996, still reverberates today with continued disappearances and torture). Thus, the literature of atrocity, in the words of critic John Treat, suffers "a nagging doubt that it may somehow constitute a moral betrayal." The "pleasure" of form, he argues, "is to be distrusted: a belief in the human instinct for form may make us think that the well-executed lyric or novel can restore coherence, through its own internal order, to even a disintegrating world."[30] Or, as Claude Lanzmann says of attempts to represent the Holocaust: "there is an absolute obscenity in the very project of understanding."[31]

Unlike Kathy Reichs, Michael Ondaatje, in his novel *Anil's Ghost,* avoids spectacular revelation and gratification. Anil, a forensic anthropologist (like the main character of *Grave Secrets*), returns to her home country, Sri Lanka, on an international human rights fact-finding mission and uncovers a skeleton that implicates the government in an extrajudicial execution. Here, however, detection and investigation lead not to a climax of clarity and repair but rather to further waiting, to the smothering of climax. Anil flees the country to avoid government detention for her damning discoveries, and the recovered body is disappeared once again, changing nothing. The ongoing, narratively monotonal work of recovery replaces the bright catharsis of validation and retribution.

Such anticlimactic narrative maneuvers, so symptomatic of the subgenre of human rights fiction, are self-conscious attempts to resist one of the basic features built into not only the novelistic form but also human rights work itself: namely, the idea that individuals have stories which run to completion—indeed, that the basic component of history is the individual's story, and that such stories, however unique, can represent their time and place, can stand in for many lives;[32] or, as this tendency manifests itself specifically in the "justice plot," that widespread crimes can be atoned for through the successful and satisfying prosecution of exemplary cases. As Anil repeats like a mantra: *"One village can speak for many villages. One victim can speak for many victims."*[33]

Such assertions are important justifications for human rights work, which needs to convince itself that its small, singular victories can achieve meaning even against heaps of unsaveable bodies. But they are also *guilty* justifications, for they celebrate a remembering that functions like forgetting. Atrocities committed against statistical arrays of faceless, nameless victims—atrocities that the author wishes to hold steadily before the reader's gaze—are often, through narrative's tendency toward individualizing empathy, funneled into the container of a single injured body. The community, as a result, is eclipsed by the wounded individual.

In a like manner, the overriding significance of the local in memorialization (it happened in *this* place, at *this* time) is often undermined by an ambient moralizing pressure toward the universal (it could be you, wherever you are, in whatever time). This pressure achieves its quintessence in the drive to allegory, represented perhaps most famously in J. M. Coetzee's *Waiting for the Barbarians,* but recognizable even in the lurid cartoonish specificity of torture novels like Stona Fitch's *Senseless.*[34] As Fitch himself wrote to me, Eliott Gast, the name of his torture-victim protagonist, is meant to signify the generality of the human: "*Gast* means 'guest' in Flemish, as in 'We are all guests in the world and should behave accordingly.' . . . A *gasthuis* is a hospital, as in 'We are all damaged and in need of healing.'"

Eric Stover, whose book *Witnesses from the Grave* was an important source for *Anil's Ghost,* describes how these collateral pressures (to focus on the one but to make that one typical) can become equally determinative, and damaging, in fieldwork. He recalled a problem that arose during his time working to uncover mass graves on behalf of the International Criminal Tribunal for the Former Yugoslavia. "The Yugoslavia Tribunal only has so many resources, and their interest is in evidence. Their interest is not necessarily in identifying everyone in a mass grave of 200 or so people. They only need a few identifications, and they need to be shown what we call characteristic evidence: that these are Bosnian Muslims, that they've got blindfolds on, hands tied behind the back—things like this, that can be used in a trial. So they weren't investing the resources into identifying everybody in the grave." As a result, he said, after sufficient evidence was collected the remains of all the leftover bodies would be turned over to local forensic authorities, who simply did not have the skills to make identifications. And the families were no closer to learning the fate of their loved ones. *"One village can speak for many villages. One victim can speak for many victims."* No trial, and no novel, can tell everyone's story, but the act of selecting a single representative (one man from the civil war in Sri Lanka, two children from the Dirty War in Argentina, one body from a grave in Vukovar) is always an erasure of many.

Such erasure is, however, the basis of coherent narration and, by some accounts, even of justice. Synecdoche and teleology are structural conditions that authors in this subgenre both rely upon and resist. When these authors manage to achieve an especially successful climax in an individual's story—when the event that the reader has been morally manipulated into desiring finally comes to pass (the torturer is shamed or killed, the kidnapped child is returned to his family)—they repeatedly, unfailingly, as if in the grip of a compulsive antinarrative tic, work to subvert the satisfaction of recompense and closure. Anne-christine d'Adesky's *Under the Bone* concludes with the liberation of a political prisoner, but only so that the woman can return to a village burned to the ground; the tortured detainee of Alan Cumyn's *Man of Bone* escapes from captivity, only to attempt suicide once he has arrived safely home. Douglas Unger's Dirty War novel *Voices from Silence* is another exemplary case, fervently discrediting the moral payoff it makes us desire. It spends nearly 300 pages building up the reader's expectations for a successful court case that will lead to official acknowledgment of the disappearances of two boys. Shortly after delivering this dramatic climax, however, it recounts how such painfully won records from the National Commission on the Disappearance of Persons are themselves being disappeared, and concludes with brute didacticism: "The world will forget."[35]

Lawrence Thornton's *Tales from the Blue Archives,* a sequel to his highly acclaimed novel of the disappeared, *Imagining Argentina,* is equally self-consuming in this sense, luring the reader along with standard devices to create narrative desire, all the while thematizing contempt for such devices. It begins by allegorizing its own need for plot and for the emotional payoff of discrete narrative advances, describing how one of its key villains, a cashiered army officer, could withstand the humiliation of his removal, but found unbearable the "days of unstructured existence [that] went on and on, one sliding into the other without differentiation."[36] Yet when the novel does deliver its discrete climax moments, it immediately, guiltily, unstructures the "differentiation" such moments deliver. After the protagonist, Dolores, wins the court case which allows her to legally retrieve her grandchildren from the Ponces (the couple that kidnapped her grandchildren after participating in the disappearance of their mother), she comforts herself with the thought that her story has reached its "end," and that this ending can serve as a reminder that "justice was still alive, breathing."[37] Such familiar courtroom drama, after all, with its finalizing verdict and its step-by-step repair of the fractured story of crimes past, is the cliché of narrative tidiness and completion. But when Dolores leaves the courtroom after the verdict, she sees the Ponces outside the courtroom standing by their truck in all their residual banality. "Dolores was surprised they had not left. She wanted the finality she had imagined, the blank screen, not their images. But it was naive to think it was over in the courtroom."

Later, after the novel has carefully structured its closure by returning to its beginning, redelivering the reader to the time of the opening pages, Dolores jarringly reflects on the meaninglessness of endings, their discontinuity with what has preceded them, or, rather, how woefully incommensurate they are to what has come before. Endings, she notes, are as cheap as soap operas. "Staring at the blank face of the television, she's reminded of the confusion when she's interrupted watching a *telenovela* and doesn't get back until it's almost over. You have the beginning and the end but no idea what went on between. If this story begins with Beatriz, what's the middle? . . . *Betrayal?* Of what? By whom?"[38] For Thornton, there is with such material a kind of deception to narrative linearity and completion. As he said when we discussed some criticism he received from an Argentinean about the perceived cathartic ending of *Imagining Argentina:* "I don't think that I could

write about this material if I thought I was going to somehow mold it toward resolution. The closure that would
bring about some kind of classical catharsis doesn't seem
to me possible. It denies both the reality of the events that
the novel is based on, and, if the novel is done right, it denies the reality of the fiction."

Ernest Gaines's *A Lesson before Dying,* Chang-rae Lee's *A
Gesture Life,* and Dave Eggers' *What Is the What* provide
three of the more ingenious solutions to this problem of
the satisfying ending that must not satisfy, the ending that
must not end. Gaines's novel is about two crimes embed-
ded within a crime. A white man is killed by two black
men; a third young black man, Jefferson, is sentenced to
death by the corrupt, racist courts simply for being present
during the shooting; and during Jefferson's trial, his lawyer
defends him by saying he is not a man, but rather a "hog,"
and thus lacks the intelligence to have planned such a murder. The verdict against Jefferson, and the dehumanizing
trial that precedes it, symbolize for his community the pervasive violations of human rights that make up the moral
background of their lives. But when the protagonist Grant
Wiggins intervenes, he does so neither to unravel the secrets of the crime and overturn the verdict, nor to shame
the courts and bring external pressure for justice. It is simply assumed that no amount of evidence could satisfy the

court, that evidence is, in such a de facto apartheid state, irrelevant. Instead, Grant intervenes to help the young man face his death with courage, like a man rather than a hog, and in that way to defy the white men who believe he will reveal the cowardliness of his race by begging for mercy or crawling at the last. The novel ends as a victory when a white guard acknowledges that Jefferson was "the bravest man in that room" on his execution day.[39] But it ends nonetheless with the execution, and with the knowledge that there can be no justice. The reader is permitted the pleasure of a redemption plot, in other words, because it is the structurally secondary redemption, and because the very pleasure of that second-class success is a shaming indicator of what we're willing to accept, what we feel must suffice, for blacks in the United States.

A Gesture Life is, likewise, a story of nested crimes that is able to move to its final, slow catharsis only because its wrenching redemption is a mere pantomime of the unredeemable. The novel is told from the perspective of Franklin Hata, a twice-displaced man (a Korean raised in racist Imperial Japan spending his final years in a racist small town in America) who can return to his home only through the haunt of memory. In the core plot, Franklin is a field medic in the Japanese army during the Pacific wars who serves as a private caregiver for one of his outpost's newly arrived "comfort girls," a young woman named Khutaeh who is essentially kidnapped from her family. He falls in love with her, rapes her, and, in what the novel depicts as a final criminal act, fails to summon the courage to kill her, allowing her instead to be gang-raped and literally ripped to pieces—her fetus torn out for Franklin to recover—by soldiers angered at her special treatment. In the container plot, decades later, these crimes are reproduced. Franklin attempts to redeem himself by adopting a young Asian orphan. Tragically, he finds himself incapable of opening himself to her love even as he yearns for it, and in an act of supreme alienation coerces her into an illegal late-term abortion which he helps to perform, effectively reenacting the disembowelment of Khutaeh. The novel ends, however, with a deftly handled and moving reconciliation between the two. It is a bare reconciliation: merely the fatigued surrender of anger by the adopted daughter, the acknowledgment of a bond with the surrendered Franklin, and the final survival of a baby, a grandchild. But this reconciliation suffices for Franklin. And it also suffices for the narrative's structural need for appropriate closure. As with *A Lesson before Dying,* it is appropriate to what precedes it precisely because it is so bare, because atonement for crimes against Khutaeh and the comfort girls throughout the Pacific is relinquished. This relinquishment is not,

in the typical formulation, an act of forgetting or abandon-
ment, but rather an acknowledgment that any narrative of
compensation would be an insult to the enormity of what
cannot be undone, and ultimately more about the well-being of the injurer rather than the injured.

Like Lee's novel, Dave Eggers' lovely and sorrowful *What
Is the What* also features parallel plots.[40] The novel inter-
weaves a grim stretch of time in the present-day life of refugee Valentino Achak Deng (he is assaulted, robbed, ne-
glected by police and doctors, and quits his job) with an
account of his horrific flight as a small child from the civil
war in Sudan. These parallel plots allow Eggers to continually lure the reader into a feeling of hope that has already
been crushed. In its final pages, the novel moves us to joy
that Deng is, at last, against all odds, about to escape the
purgatory of the Kakuma refugee camp for resettlement
in the United States. But at the same time, these final pages
are also relentless in their depiction of the heartbreak and
disappointment of his life after resettlement: Deng must
always, doggedly, continue fleeing. The great achievement
of this conclusion and this book is that these emotions do
not cancel each other out, but rather coexist as a complex
emotional palimpsest. This is possible, in part, because the
character Deng is a fictionalized version of a real person
with an imaginable future beyond the novel—the book's

proceeds will provide the real Deng the money he needs to pursue the college education he has dreamed of, and to try to rebuild his hometown. As Eggers commented, "There's good news around the bend." It's also possible because of the way the book was written. Eggers told me he wrote the section on leaving Kakuma early in their three-and-a-half-year collaboration, when he and Deng expected that Deng would soon be enrolling in college and "living the American dream." As the years passed and the setbacks and difficulties mounted, Eggers' understanding of "what Valentino had reached and what his life was really like" changed dramatically, but that early section did not. As a result, it remains suffused with the sincere euphoria of their early hope. And it is persuasive—as persuasive as the book's overall insistence that such hope for a simple and easy happy ending is naïve.

The deferral or failure of the just ending in these literary works accurately reflects the feelings of many humanitarian workers in the field. In many of my interviews, rights workers displayed keen resistance to the public's craving for clear endings to their stories, explaining not only that their time in the field was seldom sufficient to form a coherent narrative but also that the scope of most problems in principle defies such trifling enclosure. In a conversation with Edith Baeriswyl about her work as a delegate for the International Committee of the Red Cross, for instance, she mentioned a dissemination experiment she initiated in Burundi about humanitarian conduct in situations of internal violence. When I pressed her to tell me the results of the experiment, how the story ended, she said, "I left," and laughed lightly. The consequences of such work, she noted, cannot be understood in the short term—and as a Burundian woman involved in the project noted, time frames must be measured in generations: "You give birth and you educate. You keep on. That is the only way to change anything at all. We are building for the future."[41]

Many humanitarian workers thus end up, over time, experiencing their job as a frustrating way-station to justice, a series of transitions to an ever-receding good—not only because the regular geographic rotation that is designed to prevent burnout interferes with their ability to bring long-term projects to rewarding completion, but also because the role specialization that formalizes and limits human interaction often keeps workers from following the stories of individuals from beginning to end. These sharp limits to many types of missions can generate serious anxiety about consequences. What will happen after I leave? After we all leave? What will be the long-term consequences of our good intentions? "I began to think, and still do, about the

Kenyans I'd left behind," writer and former Peace Corps
staff wife Joan Richter put it in the introduction to one of
her short stories. "Gone from the scene, I could no longer
monitor their progress or their faltering, but I could wonder and hope that there would be other resources for them
to turn to, and that they would know how to find them.
My great fear was, and is, that good intentions might have
unexpected and damaging consequences."[42] When I spoke
about such intervention anxiety with former president of
Médecins Sans Frontières Rony Brauman, however, he
showed little patience for it; in such attitudes he sees not
compassion but rather arrogance. "What the people who
we help will do in the future is not our business, unless we
feel we want to go back to colonial times where we order
their lives. If we are dealing with equals they should be
able to write their own history and their own future."

Anxieties over intervention, and the arrogance of certain kinds of intervention, are expressed in human rights
fiction in a variety of ways—most notably by revealing
how representing a people's suffering can be way of *re-
ducing* them to their suffering.[43] Sarath, in *Anil's Ghost,*
harshly criticizes the international human rights workers
who visit his country: "'You know, I'd believe your arguments more if you lived here,' he said. 'You can't just slip
in, make a discovery and leave. . . . I want you to understand the archaeological surround of a fact. Or you'll be

like one of those journalists who file reports about flies
and scabs while staying at the Galle Face Hotel. That false
empathy and blame.'"[44] Dave Eggers explains how this anxiety shaped *What Is the What*.

> Early on [the manuscript] was just sort of jumping
> from headline to headline and calamity to calamity.
> I think that's a narrator's temptation, and that cer-
> tainly was Valentino's way of telling his story initially.
> He thought I was only interested in the most griev-
> ous atrocities, and so whole years would be skipped
> because "nothing of note" had happened that year in
> terms of the terrible things he had seen. [But I
> needed to] balance all the horrific parts with some
> measure of relief and calm and the other aspects of
> life, laughter and romance, all these things that make
> a full human life. If I didn't do that I would be ignor-
> ing his whole humanity, saying all he is is a product
> of statistics, all he is is somebody who's seen atroc-
> ity—there's no other aspect of his life that's of value.
> That's what I would be saying, and that's sometimes
> what we do say, unfortunately.

A doctor from *Under the Bone* expresses it with venom
when discussing human rights activists who come to Haiti:
"Why do these people from the outside only care what's

happened to us after someone dies or is murdered? . . . The only things that interest them are our reports. That's what they like—statistics. That's how they think about us—we're statistics."[45]

One of the most common ways literature thematizes the intervention anxiety dramatized in these criticisms, in which acts of care become difficult to distinguish from carelessness, is also the most extreme. In a narrative double-bind that reproduces itself in much human rights fiction, a vivid scene of abuse and interrogation, designed to mark the moral exile of the torturer, ends up operating as a device of narrative priming. In other words, the torturer's inquisition becomes an inescapable background metaphor that insinuates itself into a broad range of benign images and activities, including demonstrations of sexual desire and representations of humanitarian investigation, documentation, witnessing—even authorship itself. In such narratives, our distance from the torturer's world grows disturbingly small.

In Coetzee's *Waiting for the Barbarians*—which has become a canonical text of human rights fiction and a reference point for writers around the globe (Franklin's relationship with Khutaeh in *A Gesture Life,* for instance, seems to have been modeled upon it)—the Magistrate's ambiguously sexual, nightly massages of the unnamed young fe-

male torture survivor are a sincere if futile attempt to alle-
viate both the damage done by her interrogators and the
guilt he feels for lacking the courage to protest when he
had a chance. Yet as he massages her wounds he comes to
realize he is attempting to mark her body, to penetrate it,
in a way little different from that of her interrogators. "Is it
then the case that it is the whole woman I want, that my
pleasure in her is spoiled until these marks on her are
erased and she is restored to herself; or is it the case . . .
that it is the marks on her which drew me to her but
which, to my disappointment, I find, do not go deep
enough?"[46]

Later, reflecting upon the impotence of aging, upon his
inability to affect his young lovers, to make them feel the
coercive emotions of love, its pleasures and pains ("men of
my age . . . leave no mark of our own on the girls who
pass through our hands"),[47] his thoughts return to the scars
the "black-eyed" torturer Colonel Joll left on the barbarian
girl's body: "I must ask myself whether, when I lay head to
foot with her, fondling and kissing those broken ankles, I
was not in my heart of hearts regretting that I could not
engrave myself on her as deeply. . . . 'That is not how you
do it,' she should have said, stopping me in the act. 'If you
want to learn how to do it, ask your friend with the black
eyes.'"[48] The Magistrate's guilty intimacy eventually be-

comes a symbol of the easy deceptions of empire. The truth of authority is Colonel Joll's torture, brutal but honest, while its self-told lies are the merely gestural acts of repair that men like the Magistrate indulge in to salve their consciences—even as they continue to enjoy the benefits of imperial domination (for instance, sexual access) that are predicated upon the torture they repudiate.[49]

Similarly, in *Anil's Ghost* human rights investigators end up miming the actions of the killers they pursue in their effort to reveal the identity of a suspiciously reburied skeleton. They disturb its rest by unburying it, damage it by marking it up for identification purposes, and decapitate it to store it more securely. They lie, "kidnap" it, hide it away, and work it over in secret (lest the government intervene). When they hire a local artist to try to reconstruct what the disappeared man's face must have looked like, the final result is appalling. It becomes suddenly clear that they have created yet another head on a pole, as with so many of the retributional murders of the civil war—and the freshly traumatized painter, whose own wife was disappeared, attempts suicide.

This thematic overlap of harm and care was one of many things Clea Koff felt that *Anil's Ghost* got exactly right about the work of forensic anthropologists. In exhumations, she said, there is always the uneasy feeling that one is undoing the natural order of things, that one is a scalpel's-edge away from actions that could be seen as disrespectful to the bodies and therefore hurtful to the surviving families. Speaking of her experiences in northern Bosnia, she recalled the jolt she felt when she heard teammates discussing cases in clinical detail (a language that is "harsh," as she put it, for those not immersed in the professional context) loudly, in public spaces, in communities filled with families looking for their disappeared loved ones. She recalled how, despite the buffer of years of professional detachment, she even found herself internally flinching as she watched her team leader removing mandibles from the corpses of Rwandan children as a first step in estimating their ages, wondering to herself against her better judgment if he was using "more force than he needed to." "I used to think there was something very violent," she said, "not just about what he was doing but about what we were going to have to do." But we must *continually* do things, she said, "that in any other context would be trauma."

Throughout the literature of atrocity, authors constantly illuminate the vicious double-bind of humanitarian work: we must intervene, yet our intervention looks and feels much like injuring. In Unger's *Voices from Silence,* the protagonist, investigating the disappearances of two boys

in Argentina, finds himself deceiving a traumatized survivor he has tracked down for information: he tapes their
conversation against the man's will, even as the survivor
explains how so much of what was terrible about his political persecution was the crippling fear that he was always being spied upon, that any words he spoke could
be reported to authorities and turned against him.[50] In
d'Adesky's *Under the Bone,* the protagonist, an investigator
seeking to bring to light the experiences of women in
prison during the rule of the Duvaliers, is troubled by anxiety dreams in which her interviews violate those she
wishes to help. In one particularly striking nightmare, a
woman she interviews is strangled by her tape recorder,
which, in a precise hallucinatory logic, has become both an
instrument of electric shock and a monstrous replication
of the equipment of sexual bondage.[51] And the penulti-
mate sentence of Cumyn's *Man of Bone* is an expression of
dread from the protagonist, who has just slit his wrists,
about having to face the social worker who will try to help
him recover from his torture: ". . . pressing her pencil to
the clipboard: 'And how did it feel when they did that?
What did they do to you next? And then what?'"[52]

It is no accident that in each of these cases, as in so
many of these novels, the damage is self-referential: in
other words, the injury described is the injury entailed in
making a story. Over the years, I have sometimes assigned

to my students a novel called *Requiem for a Woman's Soul,* by Argentine journalist and human rights advocate Omar Rivabella. The book is a relentless depiction of political torture. My students have reacted to it with a range of emotions, from numb fatigue to agitated discomfort over the author's sensational use of a woman's hurt and mercilessly exposed body (it is startling to notice how many human rights fictions use an elaborately injured female body as the central narrative focus). They have written many papers about it—many, in particular, about the way the author turns the grim details of extended torture into a readable tale. Collectively they have argued that the reader's interest in Rivabella's narrowed, anguished world is maintained through several typical pleasure-and-suspense techniques: spectacular curiosity at the step-like escalation of theatrical degradation and pain as each page turns; simultaneously, a hope for the cessation of such escalation, for the possibility of final relief in the form of an escape or rescue; the guilty, voyeuristic desire to see revealed the interiors of typically hidden physical torture and sexual humiliation; and, finally, unabashed climax (it ends with the narrative equivalent of a shriek). For some undergraduates, the book is an important and effective piece of testimony. For others, it is a highly gendered pornography of pain.

What is at stake in taking human calamity as the material for a novel, in creating or reading a beautiful work of

fiction about humiliation or exposure? What does it mean
to aestheticize suffering in novels like *Waiting for the Barbar-*
ians, and what does it mean for readers to luxuriate in such
suffering in the way that, as Charles Simic once put it,
viewers linger over the elegantly excruciating torments of
martyrs in paintings? The best of these novels ask such
questions of themselves. When *Anil's Ghost,* for instance,
questions what it means for its protagonists to unbury
corpses and to subject the remains of torture victims to
curious gazes, it is also questioning what it means for an
author and a reader to do so. "Fantastic footage," the television journalist of Michael Ignatieff's *Charlie Johnson in the*
Flames says of a woman being assaulted and stripped of
her clothes by police ("the ignoble character of it only
striking him later").[53] "This is guilty art," Ignatieff commented to me, "about guilty representation." As Thornton
said when I asked about the anxieties he experienced writing *Imagining Argentina:* "I feel as if I may have intruded on
the lives of the Mothers of the Plaza de Mayo." Thornton
believes it was right to try to tell their stories—"The opposite is silence," he said—but nonetheless, as he put it, "I've
always been aware of having in effect *used* the terrible,
god-awful things that happened to these women" in attempting to testify through fiction. Thornton's comments
came back to me later in a conversation I had with William

Schulz about his work at Amnesty International USA. Amnesty knows, Schulz said, that "it can be retraumatizing for victims to be asked to tell their stories over and over again"—but this is nonetheless "something that an organization like Amnesty *depends upon* in some measure to continue to recruit people and to raise money." The perils inherent in witnessing on behalf of others, Schulz emphasized, require constant vigilance.

But even when stories of witness are not complicated by the outsider status of the storytellers, when they are controlled and written from the inside, by survivors, the moral complications of representation endure. Farnoosh Moshiri wrote her prison novel, *The Bathhouse,* almost as a form of therapy. "I began writing for myself," she told me, describing her book's relation to the torture and execution of her friends during the revolution in Iran, "basically to cure my pain, my nightmares and the linguistic block." One of the characters, a journalist who is tortured, explains that "her only desire was to survive and write about the Bathhouse. She said she was writing in her head every day and that made everything easier for her."[54] Yet at the same time that the book thematizes the moral and personal necessity of revelation, it also worries over the humiliation of exposure. The embarrassment of being seen in degradation, "being exposed,"[55] is a strong theme in *The Bathhouse*.

Countering all of these fears is the hope (recognizable sometimes only as the shadow of hope, as the resisting lament of an ill) that literature can, by expressing something true, participate in—or at the very least, as Thornton put it, act in solidarity with—the work of human rights. It is a hope that finds its most basic representation in the literature's attitude toward language itself. Important here is a strange and quite specific parallel between *Waiting for the Barbarians* and *Anil's Ghost* that reveals much about the moral stance of human rights literature. Both feature, as one of their key subplots, the attempt by a main character to translate an ancient language recently rediscovered— and both, interestingly, involve a critical moment when the translator insists to authorities that the language can be read when, in fact, it can't. These acts of translation find their thematic echo in the continual return within these texts to acts of translating across other barriers. In *Anil's Ghost:* translating the symbols readable in damaged bodies and unburied skeletons, translating bodily signals to situate oneself in a strange and hostile environment, translating the non sequiturs of a friend suffering from dementia, translating difficult texts (even if only postcards read upside-down), and translating the "lost language" between generations.[56] In *Waiting for the Barbarians:* translating or failing to translate the meaning of scars in a tortured body, translating or failing to translate overheard speech and sounds,[57] and translating or failing to translate across the language border with the barbarians ("'What a waste,' I think: 'she could have spent those long empty evenings teaching me her tongue!'").[58]

The publishing history of Ariel Dorfman's *Vuidas* (Widows) reveals one of the key sources of tension behind such thematic twitches. Dorfman planned for the novel to be translated into Danish, German, or French for its first publication, so that it might then be translated back into its original Spanish under a false name. That way he could make sure it would get past the vigilant censors who otherwise would have understood that this novel about disappearances under an imagined tyranny in Greece (and the resistance of the mothers and wives of the disappeared, who defiantly translated the bloated, rotting, unreadable faces of each recovered body into the name of a specific missing loved one) was itself a defiant translation of the history of Latin America's contemporary dictatorships.

The mute figure of Violence from Aeschylus' *Prometheus Bound*—one of the most enduring Western texts about tyranny and torture—hovers over many of these novels. At the heart of this subgenre of literature is the idea that language has been ruined, that it must be rescued. An emblematic moment occurs with one of the key disappearances in Marta Traba's *Mothers and Shadows:* "They dragged Victoria off struggling and screaming. . . . Victoria was shouting something, but I couldn't hear what. They were the last words she said to me and I couldn't hear them, can you imagine that?"[59] Edwidge Danticat's novel about a torturer from Haiti, *The Dew Breaker,* establishes its governing metaphor early, with an account of patients receiving total laryngectomies, waking from surgery bewildered at their condition, and writing panicked notes in "unsteady and hurried" script that the nurse "could not understand."[60] The violent repression documented in Tahar Djaout's *The Last Summer of Reason* culminates in the burning of books (Djaout himself was assassinated by Islamic fundamentalists before completing the novel because, as one attacker put it, he "wielded a fearsome pen that could have an effect on Islamic sectors").[61] The civilian massacre that opens Timothy Mo's *The Redundancy of Courage* reaches its climax in the killing of a journalist, and the first to be killed in Emmanuel Dongala's *Johnny Mad Dog* are the journalists. The torture and disappearances that structure Nuruddin Farah's *Sweet and Sour Milk* are generated by a subversive article that, like the disappeared notebook in Isabel Allende's *Of Love and Shadows,*[62] remains forever hidden and unread—the article, strikingly, details the elimination of all printed texts in the security apparatus of the dictatorship.[63] Lawrence Thornton's *Naming the Spirits* is about the sole survivor of a massacre during the Dirty War in Argentina who has lost her capacity for language; and in a crucial moment of *Imagining Argentina* the protagonist, searching for his disappeared wife, encounters a woman whose tongue was cut out at Auschwitz.[64] Omar Rivabella's *Requiem for a Woman's Soul* is, in its entirety, the record of an attempt to translate into a coherent, linear memoir the disjointed and sometimes unreadable sentences by a woman named Susana, written shakily in blood and feces on scraps of tissue and toilet paper, that are smuggled out of the detention center (the book concludes with the translator, Father Antonio, driven to insanity and mumbling "unintelligible words").[65] Michael Ignatieff's *Charlie Johnson in the Flames* is threaded throughout with images of lost language. It opens with a civilian woman, set on fire by a Serbian colonel, moaning inarticulately; at midpoint, video footage of the woman is revealed that shows her opening and closing her mouth in failed words as she burns; at the conclusion, the man seeking justice for her is killed when confronting the perpetrator, his "last word" as inarticulate as her original moaning. This failed language, like hers, is captured on a tape, which is then burned by grieving friends who don't wish to hear.[66] In *Guantánamo: Honor Bound to Defend Freedom,* a play by Victoria Brittain and Gillian Slovo, the US military censors letters, euphemizes interrogation as "exhibition" and interrogators as "investigators," and officially reclassifies suicide by detainees as "manipulative self-injurious behavior" (to avoid the bad press of multiple monthly suicide attempts).[67] As the poet-protagonist of Hong Ying's *Summer of Betrayal* writes after fleeing Tiananmen Square: "Everything that I narrate / seems to have lost its meaning."[68]

Achieving clear language is, indeed, experienced as just such a crisis in the human rights community, from the most abstract to the most visceral levels. Maurice Blanchot discusses how disaster, epitomized in the Holocaust, reveals the emptiness of all language;[69] Marguerite Feitlowitz tracks the systemic damage authoritarian regimes inflict on communication ("I have come to believe that, even after the regime has ended, language may be the last system to recover");[70] and Elaine Scarry explains how pain, epitomized in torture, is virtually incommunicable and reduces us to the pre-language of cries and grunts.[71] Language is a problem at even the most quotidian levels. Those working in the field, for instance, seldom have the opportunity to work in their first language—a problem reproduced in the fiction itself, which often must be accessed in translation, or written in a second language in order to reach, as author Farnoosh Moshiri said to me, the people who don't already know these stories. Gilbert Holleufer, a delegate from the ICRC, explains some of the problems in fieldwork that occur with translation and retranslation across cultures. Describing his work preparing the ICRC's worldwide survey of humanitarian mores, the "People on War" Project, he noted in an interview with me:

> We listed words that are dynamite in some contexts, and we had to go through a long process here to adapt the vocabulary, the semantics of these questionnaires, to make them palatable in the context. . . . In the Philippines, for instance, you don't speak about "conflict" and "war" and things like this—you speak about "encounters." . . . [For instance,] we are using words like "victimization." Now imagine what a Rwandan citizen may think when he reads or hears internationals talking about what he has been going through in terms of victimization. Isn't this humiliating? The language disincarnates, it disembodies reality, and they know it. They know that we are disembodying their reality, we are dissolving it into words. . . . Humanitarian language is part of the feeling of threat they have.

Holleufer continued by explaining that translation problems run through every level of behavior in humanitarian work.

Humanitarian semantics can defeat the purpose
sometimes. [For instance,] in many cultures you cannot accept a gift if you can't reciprocate. This is the
way they are living, their ordinary everyday life, and
suddenly they are stuck in a situation where they
are so hungry, they are so defeated, so failed, that
they need to be assisted. And then come trucks that
distribute in numbers, and then you get your bowl of
rice. And you were a proud man, or a proud woman,
being maybe the daughter of the chief of the village.
So the language of behavior is important. You know
how Hezbollah assists their people? They come at
night, hooded, with the family parcel. What's in
there is the same as the ICRC—you can't change it,
you have to bring food. But they knock at the door
very discreetly, and they come hooded, and they say
just one sentence of the Koran, very formal, nothing personal, hand it over, and they disappear in the
night. It's totally anonymous, and nobody in the village knows who is assisted. And the United Nations
comes with a big truck in the middle of the village,
cameras, and all this. Let's think about it. Language is
not only words.

Given such realities, it is unsurprising that so many of
these books are fixated on the problem of how to commu-

nicate in a fractured world. *Under the Bone* is concerned, throughout, with the difficulties international human rights activists face working in Haiti with imperfect Creole. *Voices from Silence* is almost obsessive in its continual emphasis on the mundane necessity of translating between the many characters who don't share a language—a literary echo of the real-world experiences of women like Renée Epelbaum, a mother of the Plaza de Mayo, who said of the junta's pervasive and distorting rhetoric: "It made you *psychotic*. We could barely 'read,' let alone 'translate' the world around us. And that was exactly what they wanted."[72] *Red Dust* is even more relentless in its depictions of silence, which is the opposite of translation, or the mark of its failure: by the end of the book, "silence" is almost a verbal tic, with some extended sections using the word on every page. "Language is inadequate," Gillian Slovo explained when we discussed this, "to represent such experiences that were so awful they seem to defy normal understanding."

While such lament over linguistic fracture is the more typical approach in this subgenre, a cluster of texts offer a striking representational alternative. The plot of Thornton's *Naming the Spirits,* for instance, is ultimately a plot of recovery, its aphasic protagonist moving into speech like an infant, toddling over sounds and names and clattering her way to a painfully earned second chance at language.

"Speech," Thornton says, "lifts the veil." And at the spiritual center of *A Lesson before Dying* is the almost illegible diary of the partly literate character Jefferson. Through this act of writing, Jefferson achieves a sense of self and connection with his family that helps him and, by extension, his entire community recover the feeling of dignity that was stripped from them by the racist courts that sentenced him to death. Ann Patchett's lyric novel *Bel Canto,* about a group of international travelers held hostage by guerrillas in the home of the vice-president of an unidentified South American country, uses what might be called a mirror plot to develop its fundamental concern with language. Outside, the multilingual ICRC delegate works to bring about nonviolent reconciliation between the security forces and the guerrillas by translating their reciprocal demands, while inside the multilingual translator brings about the smaller, more personal reconciliations of the bewildered hostages by translating throughout all their interpersonal dramas and budding romances. While the novel gives due attention to the strenuous, negative labor of translation with the outside (our linguistic isolation will bring violence if we do not overcome it), the heart of its interest is on the lovely inverse of the inside (our linguistic isolation can be overcome by a care and creativity that models, in its simple beauty, a reason for nonviolence).

Bel Canto examines with rich, celebratory detail the he-

roic attempts of lonely individuals to build a shared language—a language that can unite not only across the barriers of mother tongues but also across the barriers of fear
and violence, even bridging the emotional and moral distance between hostages and hostage takers. The disarm-
ing, childlike patience of pidgin communication functions
in almost melodic counterpoint to the sudden bursts of
clarity provided by competent translation, and these in
turn play in radiant tones against the transcendentally uni-
fying experiences of understanding through the "universal" languages of music and chess. The novel's outside
ends in a crush of violence ("the men were shouting something, but with . . . the deafness left over from the gunfire,
not even Gen [the translator] could understand them"),[73]
but the last words go to the inside plot, in an epilogue that
offers redemption through an interracial, interlinguistic
marriage between two of the hostages.

In *The Body in Pain,* Elaine Scarry writes with quiet
passion about the capacity of language to rebuild worlds
broken by violence. She notes in particular how in prison
camps around the world the barest achievements of communication can be a startling triumph over the "unthinkable isolation" of torture:

> The prisoner who, alone in long solitary confinement
> and repeatedly tortured, found within a loaf of bread

a matchbox containing a small piece of paper that had written on it the single, whispered word "Corragio!", "Take courage"; the Uruguayan man arranging for some tangible signal that his words had reached their destination, "My darling, if you receive this letter put a half a bar of Boa soap in the next parcel"; the imprisoned Chilean women who on Christmas Eve sang with all their might to their men in a separate camp the song they had written, "Take heart, Jose, my love" and who, through the abusive shouts of guards ordering silence, heard "faintly on the wind . . . the answering song of the men"—these acts and their multiplication in the extensive and ongoing attempts of Amnesty International to restore to each person tortured his or her voice, to use language to let pain give an accurate account of itself, to present regimes that torture with a deluge of letters and telegrams, a deluge of voices speaking on behalf of, voices speaking in the voice of, the person silenced, these acts that return to the prisoner his most elemental political ground as well as his psychic content and density, are finally almost physiological in their power of alteration. As torture consists of acts that magnify the way in which pain destroys a person's world, self, and voice, so these other acts that

restore the voice become not only a denunciation of
the pain but almost a diminution of the pain, a partial reversal of the process of torture itself.[74]

Perhaps the most dramatic literary emblems for each
model of language implicit in this passage—language as
fragile and endangered, language as powerful and capa-
cious—come from *Requiem for a Woman's Soul.* The brutally tortured Susana describes an instant from her detention: "I was sitting on my bed when the peephole was
opened briefly and a wad of paper was thrown in, rolling almost to my feet. I unfolded it carefully. The words,
'Bravery and Courage' were written on it. The world
seemed so marvelous to me that I began to weep. I read
it and reread it a hundred times."[75] But this moment of
great pathos and hope—my students have reported weep-
ing over Susana's discovery of the note, at the depth of
need that humble message filled—stands in stark contrast
to the book's concluding image: Susana's hands (the hands
she wrote with, the hands she used to pass on and receive
her messages) cut off at the wrists and delivered to her father like a letter.

I'd like to close this book where it began, with a story from Rwanda—a story whose telling raises important questions about many of the issues that have structured this book: the physical and moral risks of professional witnessing; the difference it makes; the simultaneous suspicion of and yearning for therapeutic narrative closure; the nature of hope.

Donatella Lorch was taken to the Mille Collines Hotel in Kigali by an ICRC convoy at the height of the killings (Belgian troops had already come to evacuate the foreigners at the hotel and refused to come again, so Roméo Dallaire arranged a personal escort to evacuate her and the other journalists who remained behind). Images of what Lorch saw during the genocide still shake her; the fact that she was able to leave when so many could not still gnaws at her. "Most of the Mille Collines refugees just stood and stared as we left," she wrote in a message to me. "I remember one woman in particular, she was Eastern European and was married to a Tutsi, coming into my room the night before we left to beg us to save her husband and smuggle him out to the airport. I know we all wanted to figure out ways to smuggle people out but the UN was adamant that we were not allowed. I understood why as we made out way out of the hotel. The interahamwe searched our cars thoroughly and I have no doubt would have turned on everybody if they had found a Rwandan. I still have no words to describe what it feels like to tell someone 'I'm sorry I can't try to save you.' Does that make me a coward? Yes."

Even now, more than a decade later, retriggered memories can feel like a physical blow to her. But when we talked with each other about it, the memory Lorch shared that seemed most vivid for her was not about the terrible things she saw then—the corpses piled in heaps, the people watching her leave, the Interahamwe threatening her—but rather about something that happened afterward.

When Lorch returned to the United States, she felt very lonely. "Even then, Rwanda was the name of a place very few people recognized. I think that isolated me; I felt I couldn't share my experiences with people." The *New York Times,* where she was still the bureau chief for East Africa, asked her to see a staff psychiatrist. "The psychiatrist asked me all these questions about how I was feeling, how I was adapting, and then she turned to me and asked: 'So what happened in Rwanda anyway?' And I thought to myself, what am I wasting my time here for?"

Lorch remembers the precise moment when things started to change for her, when she found herself able to begin moving forward again. As in 1993, when four friends she was working with in Somalia were killed by an angry crowd, the recovery started with a small act of storytelling. Almost a year after the genocide, she found herself in Kigali again, sitting on a broken ledge in what had once been an Officers' Club. The place was ruined, but the sun was on her back and there was music playing and people were dancing. She was writing a story about weddings in Rwanda. "There was suddenly this wave of weddings," she told me. "So many people were getting married in churches that couples were getting married two or three in one go. One ceremony, then the next, then the next—you would have four or five ceremonies in a day."

"For some, there is a deeply felt urgency to get married," she wrote in the article. "Wellars Bizimuremyi, 40, lost his wife, child and entire family to the massacres. Two weeks ago he met a young woman who had also lost everyone and immediately proposed. They plan to marry at the end of the month. 'You have to rebuild your life,' Mr. Bizimuremyi said. 'I want to start a family again. Otherwise, what do I live for?'"[1]

For Lorch, being invited to the wedding party at the Officers' Club that night, seeing people celebrating—it was one of the most remarkable changes in landscape one could imagine. "It was this desire to continue life," she said. "Just to continue life."

1. Two clarifying comments. First, while it is customary to speak of a global human rights movement, this is of course only a shorthand way of referring to a complex organizational array and a multifaceted discourse operating in different ways in a variety of cultures. As Upendra Baxi puts it: "There is not *one* world of 'human rights' but many conflicting worlds" (Baxi, *The Future of Human Rights* [Oxford: Oxford University Press, 2002], p. 5).

Second, throughout this book I repeatedly refer to "humanitarian and human rights work" without drawing attention each time to the customary distinctions between "humanitarian" and "human rights" endeavors. Though the legal traditions behind the two have recently begun to converge, the terms initially marked a distinction between laws applied to armed conflict and laws designed to protect individuals in both war and peace. For more on this topic, see

International Committee of the Red Cross, "International Humanitarian Law and International Human Rights Law: Similarities and Differences," www.icrc.org (accessed 15 June 2006); and David Forsythe, *The Humanitarians: The International Committee of the Red Cross* (Cambridge: Cambridge University Press, 2005), pp. 250–259. Discussion of distinctions between the two categories can also proceed by focusing on special terms (like "neutrality" or "agency") or by attempting to contrast the relative scope of their ambitions. David Forsythe, a political-science professor who has published extensively on human rights, offered me this explanation for thinking about the terms:

"No doubt some people think of human rights in terms of law and litigation, while thinking of humanitarian affairs in terms of diplomacy and various services. This is not entirely correct, first of all because the idea of human rights can lead not only to hard law (adjudicated law via courts) but also to soft law in the form of extra-judicial politics, diplomacy, services, and education. Secondly, humanitarian affairs can entail attention to law in various forms—as in the adjudication of international humanitarian law in various courts.

"As for humanitarian affairs considered by itself,

there is no one definition or approach or tradition that is dominant or always accepted. One longstanding approach is that of the Red Cross (Red Crescent). This approach to humanitarianism emphasizes neutrality, impartiality, and independence from states, their intergovernmental organizations, and their power politics. But at least in theory there is a less neutral, more engaged approach that tries to both provide various humanitarian services such as medical assistance, while blowing the whistle on human rights violations or the root causes of humanitarian distress [here Forsythe references Médecins Sans Frontières (Doctors Without Borders)].

"There are a number of people and organizations who think of 'humanitarian' in terms of emergency protection (including relief or assistance) in response to exceptional distress. So one has humanitarian action not only in war, but also in response to tsunamis or other national disasters. The International Federation of Red Cross and Red Crescent Societies defines its primary focus as responding to national and industrial/technological disasters. So the notion of emergency response in exceptional situations is often associated with 'humanitarianism.'

"One might very well question why the international

community should pay special attention to those in dire straits because of war or natural disaster, when others are in equally dire straits because of the failures of development. Nevertheless, for some, there is a difference between disaster relief ('humanitarian'), and chronic hunger and infant mortality (a matter of underdevelopment). One speaks of humanitarian agencies for exceptional relief, and development agencies to fight hunger and infant mortality in 'normal' times.

"Some agencies like UNICEF (or Oxfam among the NGOs) do both emergency relief and development programming. UNICEF can also be analyzed as more and more introducing human rights notions into its work, especially after the extensive ratification of the UN Convention on the Rights of the Child. So what UNICEF may have previously been content to call its regular development work for mothers and children it now also refers to in terms of the human rights of mothers and children.

"In general there has been, at the UN Development Program and related NGOs and IGOs, an effort to introduce human rights concepts into 'development,' blurring the distinctions between human rights and development. Of course the UN General

Assembly has passed a nonbinding resolution endorsing a people's collective human right to development.

"There has also been a blurring of the distinctions between human rights and humanitarian law/diplomacy. Given some of the language in the two 1977 additional protocols to the 1949 Geneva Conventions for victims of war, one can speak of an individual right to learn the fate of a relative detained by a fighting party, or a family member who is missing. So humanitarian law, made by and for states primarily, entails explicitly or implicitly some individual rights. For example, the ICRC in international armed conflict has a right to visit detainees, but this can be interpreted to mean that combatant and civilian prisoners have a right to talk to an ICRC representative.

"So the semantic and conceptual and other boundaries to terms like (1) 'humanitarian,' (2) 'development,' or (3) 'human rights' are very much subjective and in flux, subjected to different uses in different contexts."

2. *Lettres sans frontières,* ed. Roger Job (Brussels: Editions Complexe, 1994), p. 69 (ICRC translation).

3. Sir Philip Sidney, *An Apology for Poetry,* ed. Forrest Robinson (Indianapolis: Bobbs-Merrill, 1970), p. 46.

4. Theodor Adorno, "Commitment," in *The Essential Frankfurt School Reader,* ed. Andrew Arato and Eike Gebhardt, introduction by Paul Piccone (New York: Continuum, 1982), pp. 312–313. On readings and misreadings of Adorno's comment, see Michael Rothberg, "After Adorno: Culture in the Wake of Catastrophe," *New German Critique* 72 (Autumn 1997): 45–48.

5. Antjie Krog, *Country of My Skull* (New York: Three Rivers Press, 1998), p. 312.

6. Garentina Kraja, quoted in Ardian Arifaj, "Does Journalism Matter? After the War in Kosova, Albanian Reporters Reassess Their Work," *Nieman Reports* 54, no. 2 (Summer 2000): 81.

7. See, for instance, *From Massacres to Genocide: The Media, Public Policy, and Humanitarian Crises,* ed. Robert Rotberg and Thomas Weiss (Washington, D.C.: Brookings Institution, 1996); Mustapha Masmoudi, "The New Information World Order," *Journal of Communication* 29, no. 2 (Spring 1979): 172–179; Tsan-Kuo Chang, Pamela Shoemaker, and Nancy Brendlinger, "Determinants of International News Coverage in the U.S. Media," *Communication Research* 14, no. 4 (August 1987): 396–414; and Edward Girardet, "Public Opinion, the Media, and Humanitarianism,"

in *Humanitarianism across Borders: Sustaining Civilians in Times of War*, ed. Thomas Weiss and Larry Minear (Boulder: Lynn Rienner, 1993), pp. 39–56.

8. Rony Brauman, former president of Médecins Sans Frontières, recalls how an MSF mission to the Kurdish villages gassed on the orders of Saddam Hussein received "little press coverage, despite the images it brought back; at the time, he had been a friend to the West, the rampart containing fundamentalist Islam within Iran." Brauman concludes: "Victims of a tyrant only become 'victims' when the tyrant has been perceived and labeled as such by Western governments." See Brauman, "When Suffering Makes a Good Story," in *Life, Death and Aid: The Médecins Sans Frontières Report on World Crisis Intervention*, ed. François Jean (London: Routledge, 1993), p. 155.

9. John Conroy, *Unspeakable Acts, Ordinary People: The Dynamics of Torture* (New York: Alfred A. Knopf, 2000), pp. 244–247. Stanley Cohen lists a number of obstacles to the successful dissemination of human rights information: outright denial of injury ("The media is lying"); denial that the injured should be regarded as victims ("We have injured them, but they are terrorists and we are defending ourselves"); denial of responsibility ("Atrocities were committed, but by un-

known forces or third groups rather than the government"); condemnation of the condemners ("Those accusing us are corrupt, biased, or hypocritical"); and appeal to higher loyalty ("Our actions are necessary to protect our nation, our revolution, our purity"). See Stanley Cohen, *Denial and Acknowledgment: The Impact of Information about Human Rights Violations* (Jerusalem: Hebrew University, 1995), pp. 33–35, 71–84.

10. Cohen, *Denial and Acknowledgment*, pp. 35, 47. On bystander intervention, see Bibb Latané and John Darley, *The Unresponsive Bystander: Why Doesn't He Help?* (New York: Appleton-Century-Crofts, 1970); also Jane Allyn Piliavin, John Dovidio, Samuel Gaertner, and Russell Clark, *Emergency Intervention* (New York: Academic Press, 1981).

11. Peter Maass, *Love Thy Neighbor: A Story of War* (New York: Alfred A. Knopf, 1996), p. 115.

12. Michael Maren, *The Road to Hell: The Ravaging Effects of Foreign Aid and International Charity* (New York: Free Press, 1997), pp. 2–3.

13. See Elliot Sober and David Wilson, *Unto Others: The Evolution and Psychology of Unselfish Behavior* (Cambridge, Mass.: Harvard University Press, 1998).

14. See, for instance, Fiona Terry, *The Paradox of Humani-*

tarian Action (Ithaca: Cornell University Press, 2002), p. 231. Raymond Bonner, reviewing Maren's sharp criticisms of humanitarian aid organizations, reveals another dismaying consequence of the need to be seen: during the refugee crisis in Rwanda, he writes, "more than 100 humanitarian groups invaded, creating the most indecorous scenes of public relations officers shouting and pushing to get their group on television or into a newspaper, and bad-mouthing the work of competing charities." Bonner, "Bad Samaritans," *New York Times Book Review*, 23 March 1997, p. 23.

15. David Kennedy, *The Dark Sides of Virtue: Reassessing International Humanitarianism* (Princeton: Princeton University Press, 2004), pp. 24–25.

16. Mary Anderson, "'You Save My Life Today, But for What Tomorrow?': Some Moral Dilemmas of Humanitarian Aid," in *Hard Choices: Moral Dilemmas in Humanitarian Intervention*, ed. Jonathan Moore (Oxford: Rowman and Littlefield, 1998), p. 145.

17. Rony Brauman, "From Philanthropy to Humanitarianism: Remarks and an Interview," trans. Sarah Clift, *SAQ: South Atlantic Quarterly* 103, nos. 2–3 (Spring–Summer 2004), p. 400.

18. Terry, *The Paradox of Humanitarian Action*, pp. 1–54.

19. Quoted in Adam Shatz, "Mission Impossible: Humanitarianism Is Neutral or It Is Nothing," Médecins Sans Frontières, 20 October 2002, available at www.msf.org (accessed 8 September 2005).

1. GENOCIDE

1. François Mitterrand, quoted in an article by Patrick Saint-Exupéry and Charles Lambroschini, *Le Figaro*, 12 January 1998.

2. Roméo Dallaire, with Brent Beardsley, *Shake Hands with the Devil: The Failure of Humanity in Rwanda* (New York: Carroll and Graf, 2004), p. 499.

3. Boubacar Boris Diop, "African Authors in Rwanda: Writing by Duty of Memory," trans. Jane Hale, in *Literary Responses to Mass Violence,* conference papers (Waltham, Mass.: Brandeis University, 2004), p. 111.

4. *Rwanda: Death, Despair and Defiance* (London: African Rights, 1994), pp. 352, 350.

5. Philip Gourevitch, "Conversations with History," an interview at the Institute of International Studies, University of California at Berkeley, 11 February 2000. Available at globetrotter.berkeley.edu/people (accessed 20 April 2007).

6. Many thanks to the translators and transcribers who facilitated my conversation with Diop: Joelle Vitiello, Charles Sugnet, and Sébastien Saunoi-Sandgren.

7. Boubacar Boris Diop, "Writing by Duty of Memory," a talk given at Macalester College, St. Paul, Minnesota, 12 April 2005.

8. Ibid.

9. Ibid.

10. *Kirkus Reviews,* 1 July 1999.

11. Stanley Péan, "Bye Bye 2000," *La Presse,* 31 December 2000.

12. Gil Courtemanche, *A Sunday at the Pool in Kigali,* trans. Patricia Claxton (New York: Alfred A. Knopf, 2003), pp. 245, 249.

13. Ibid., p. 246.

14. Ibid., p. 259.

15. "When Truth Is Plainer in Fiction," *The Age,* 9 August 2003. Available at www.theage.com.au (accessed 8 September 2005).

16. Courtemanche, *A Sunday at the Pool in Kigali,* p. 217. The novel, to be fair, is anxious about its relative artlessness, imagining its own settings as reminiscent of "C-grade-movie" settings (41), and featuring characters who complain about "heavy-handed soap opera" plots (16) and who admit to those they are talking to (and to the reader) that their clumsy informational monologues are much like the lectures of "a tourist guide" (126).

17. *Rwanda: Death, Despair and Defiance,* pp. 749–750.

18. Quoted in Arthur Kleinman and Joan Kleinman, "Cultural Appropriations of Suffering in Our Times," in *Social Suffering,* ed. Arthur Kleinman, Veena Das, and Margaret Lock (Berkeley: University of California Press, 1997), p. 23.

19. Ibid., p. 19.

20. Philip Gourevitch prompts readers to be aware of such references; see *We Wish to Inform You That Tomorrow We Will Be Killed with Our Families: Stories from Rwanda* (New York: Picador, 1998), pp. 184, 284. See also Guy Lawson, "Sorrows of a Hero," *New York Review of Books,* 26 May 2005, p. 35.

21. Courtemanche, *A Sunday at the Pool in Kigali,* p. 115.

22. Ibid., p. 224.

23. Dallaire "douses himself with Brut" and has a "salesman's moustache" (ibid., pp. 14–15). A footnote explains that ten Belgian Blue Berets were murdered as the genocide began and that Dallaire "made no attempt to free them."

24. Kofi Annan, Remarks, International Rescue Committee's Freedom Award Dinner, New York, 10 November 2004, www.un.org (accessed 8 September 2005).

25. Testimony of Roméo Dallaire, in *The Prosecutor of the Tribunal v. Théoneste Bagosora, Anatole Nsengiyuma, Gratien Kabaligi, and Aloys Ntabakuze,* International

Criminal Tribunal for Rwanda, 20 January 2004, pp. 31–32.

26. *Rwanda: Death, Despair and Defiance*, p. 336.

27. Ibid., pp. 237–238. One notable exception was a telephone at the Hôtel des Mille Collines, of which extremists were unaware. Its effectiveness in saving lives (dramatically represented in the movie *Hotel Rwanda*) underscores the importance of the communication-cutting strategies of the génocidaires.

28. Dina Temple-Raston, *Justice on the Grass: Three Rwandan Journalists, Their Trial for War Crimes, and a Nation's Quest for Redemption* (New York: Free Press, 2005), p. 237.

29. The phrase is from Elaine Scarry, *The Body in Pain: The Making and the Unmaking of the World* (New York: Oxford University Press, 1985), p. 131. For a powerful analysis of this process in Argentina's Dirty War (1976–1983), see Marguerite Feitlowitz, *A Lexicon of Terror: Argentina and the Legacies of Torture* (Oxford: Oxford University Press, 1998).

30. *Rwanda: Death, Despair and Defiance*, p. 166.

31. Ibid., p. 243.

32. Ibid., pp. 243, 63.

33. Ibid., p. 247.

34. Ibid., pp. 245–246.

35. Ibid., p. 251.

36. Gourevitch, *We Wish to Inform You That Tomorrow We Will Be Killed with Our Families*, p. 39.

37. Ibid., pp. 156, 185–186.

38. Ibid., p. 153.

39. *Rwanda: Death, Despair and Defiance*, p. 100.

40. Ibid., p. 218.

41. Ibid., pp. 569–570.

42. See, for instance, Paul Greenberg, "Rot at the Top," *Washington Times*, Commentary, 8 April 2005.

43. Samantha Power, introduction to Roméo Dallaire, *Shake Hands with the Devil: The Failure of Humanity in Rwanda* (New York: Carroll and Graf, 2004), p. ix.

44. See, for instance, *The Prosecutor of the Tribunal v. Théoneste Bagosora et al.*, International Criminal Tribunal for Rwanda, 19 January 2004, p. 87, and 20 January 2004, p. 26.

45. Ibid., 27 January 2004, p. 37.

46. Ibid., 26 January 2004, p. 20.

47. Ibid., 5 February 2004, p. 11.

48. Ibid., 26 January 2004, p. 57.

49. Ibid., 20 January 2004, p. 30.

50. Ibid., 21 January 2004, p. 75.

51. Ibid., 26 January 2004, p. 62.

52. Ibid., 27 January 2004, p. 19.

53. Peter Erlinder, "Behind the Scenes at the Hotel Rwanda," a talk given at Mayday Books, Minneapolis, Minnesota, 6 March 2005.

54. I am not a lawyer, but the prosecution of Nazi leader Klaus Barbie seems to me at least indirectly relevant here. In 1985, the French high court held that Barbie's responsibility for crimes against the Resistance was not subject to statutory limitation, because he could be charged with crimes against humanity (targeting civilians and ethnic groups) rather than war crimes (use of prohibited force against combatants) even though members of the Resistance were combatants. The court argued that the "'heinous' crimes . . . were presented, by those in whose name they were perpetrated, as justified politically by the National Socialist ideology." In other words, the status of the victims was less important than the intent of the perpetrators. See "Barbie," in *International Law Reports*, vol. 78 (London: Butterworth, 1988), pp. 139–140.

55. *Rwanda: Death, Despair and Defiance*, pp. 778, 337; *The Prosecutor of the Tribunal v. Ferdinand Nahimana, Hassan Ngeze, Jean-Bosco Barayagwiza*, International Criminal Tribunal for Rwanda, 24 October 2000, p. 144.

56. Dallaire, *Shake Hands with the Devil*, p. 312.

57. For Gourevitch's own account of the scavenging dogs, see *We Wish to Inform You That Tomorrow We Will Be Killed with Our Families*, pp. 147–149.

58. David Stoll's research is described in David Horowitz, "I, Rigoberta Menchú, Liar," *Salon*, 11 January 1999.

59. Kay Schaffer and Sidonie Smith, *Human Rights and Narrated Lives: The Ethics of Recognition* (New York: Palgrave Macmillan, 2004), pp. 31–32.

60. One study argues that people are less likely to respond to requests for help from charitable organizations when "the extent and persistence" of the need situation is accentuated. In other words, because people are less likely to feel that their contribution can help change a chronic situation, they are less likely to try. See Peter Warren and Iain Walker, "Empathy, Effectiveness and Donations to Charity: Social Psychology's Contribution," *British Psychological Society* 30 (1991): 325–337.

61. The phrase is from Gillian Whitlock, *The Intimate Empire: Reading Women's Autobiography* (London: Cassell, 2000), p. 146.

62. Quoted in Feitlowitz, *A Lexicon of Terror*, p. 35.

63. Relatedly, see Betty Plewes and Rieky Stuart, "The Pornography of Poverty: a Cautionary Fundraising

Tale," in *Ethics in Action: The Ethical Challenges of International Human Rights Nongovernmental Organizations,* ed. Daniel Bell and Jean-Marc Coicaud (Cambridge: Cambridge University Press, 2007), pp. 23–37; see also Jonathan Benthall, *Disasters, Relief and the Media* (London: I. B. Tauris, 1993), pp. 179–186.

64. There are various techniques for maximizing the effectiveness of requests for aid. One study by B. Latané and J. M. Jackson even suggests "that complying with a charitable request may be more a function of the immediate situational pressures associated with such a request than a function of altruism." (Quoted in Bill Thornton, Gayle Kirchner, and Jacqueline Jacobs, "Influence of a Photograph on a Charitable Appeal: A Picture May Be Worth a Thousand Words When It Has To Speak for Itself," *Journal of Applied Social Psychology* 21, no. 6 [1991]: 433, referring to J. M. Jackson and B. Latané, "Strength and Number of Solicitors and the Urge toward Altruism," *Personality and Social Psychology Bulletin* 7 [1981]: 415–422.)

Consider psychologically robust techniques of persuasion such as the foot-in-the-door effect. In one study, for instance, students asked to sign a letter to the president emphasizing the need for assistance to the homeless were significantly more likely than those not previously contacted to agree to a larger request later on to take part in a food drive for the homeless. One of many such studies, it explains the amplification of altruism as the result of our need to maintain consistent self-perception ("My previous actions show that I am an altruistic person who cares about this issue; such a person would comply with this new, larger request"). Other studies, however, reveal a reverse foot-in-the-door effect. If, for instance, there is an inadequate delay between requests, significant resistance can be generated ("I have already done my share"). See Jerry M. Burger, "Self-Concept Clarity and the Foot-in-the-Door Procedure," *Basic and Applied Social Psychology* 25, no. 1 (2003): 79–86; and Rosanna E. Guadagno, Terrilee Asher, Linda J. Demaine, and Robert B. Cialdini, "When Saying Yes Leads to Saying No: Preference for Consistency and the Reverse Foot-in-the-Door Effect," *Personality and Social Psychology Bulletin* 27, no. 7 (July 2001): 859–867.

Analyzing persuasion at a more abstract level, Alison Brysk tracks the evolution of human rights by summarizing the features that make new and emerging moral norms more likely to succeed. "New norms are more quickly and widely accepted when they: resonate with core principles of modernity such as equality and progress, appeal for physical protection of vulnerable groups, develop naturally from preexisting principles, follow a catalyzing historical event, and are articulated by transformational leaders—individuals or groups possessing 'moral capital'" (Brysk, *Human Rights and Private Wrongs* [New York: Routledge, 2005], p. 22). See, relatedly, Jeri Laber, *The Courage of Strangers* (New York: Public Affairs, 2002), pp. 73, 170, for Laber's account of the "successful formula" she used at Helsinki Watch for reporting abuses.

65. Fiona Terry, *The Paradox of Humanitarian Action* (Ithaca: Cornell University Press, 2002), p. 231.

66. William Shawcross, "The Numbing of Humanity: Have We Had One Atrocity Too Many?" *Washington Post*, National Weekly Edition, September 1984, p. 23.

67. At the time I was writing this book, Koff was in the process of founding a nonprofit organization called the Missing Persons Identification Resource Center. According to its website, the organization was "formed to support families and friends of missing persons. MPID aims to improve the quality and quantity of information on missing persons by joining with their relatives and friends to build anthro-

pological profiles of the missing. MPID anticipates that such profiles will improve the probability that law enforcement will generate matches between missing and unidentified persons both living and dead. MPID's doors are not yet open, as fundraising is underway for the first year's budget." MPID's services will be free to friends and relatives of the missing. See www.mpid.org (accessed 6 February 2006).

68. Clea Koff, *The Bone Woman: A Forensic Anthropologist's Search for Truth in the Mass Graves of Rwanda, Bosnia, Croatia, and Kosovo* (New York: Random House, 2004), p. 7.

69. Ibid., pp. 5, 13, 16.

70. Ibid., p. 17.

71. Ibid., p. 46.

72. World Health Organization, "Mortality Projections for Darfur," www.who.int (accessed 8 September 2005).

73. Nicholas Kristof, "When Genocide Is a Story Left Largely Untold," *Nieman Reports* 59, no. 2 (Summer 2005): 112.

74. Ibid., p. 113.

75. Nathalie Civet, Médecins Sans Frontières Head of Mission in Sudan, United Nations Security Council "Arria Formula" meeting, 27 July 2005. Available at www.msf.org (accessed 8 September 2005).

76. Caroline Moorehead, "Letter from Darfur," *New York Review of Books* 52, no. 13 (11 August 2005): 56.

2. INTERROGATION

1. "Convention Relating to the Status of Refugees, Adopted on 28 July 1951 by the United Nations Conference of Plenipotentiaries on the Status of Refugees and Stateless Persons Convened under General Assembly Resolution 429(V) of 14 December 1950; Entry into Force 22 April 1954," Chapter 1, Article 1, Section A(2). See Office of the UN High Commissioner for Human Rights, www.ohchr.org/english/law/refugees.htm.

2. MSF personnel who stayed, writes David Forsythe, had to be incorporated into the ICRC delegation and don their emblem in order to avoid attack. See David Forsythe, *The Humanitarians: The International Committee of the Red Cross* (Cambridge: Cambridge University Press, 2005), pp. 122–123.

3. For a fuller discussion of the ICRC's confidentiality policies, see ibid., pp. 69, 138, 194, 295–302.

4. Nelson Mandela, British Red Cross Humanity Lecture, London, 11 July 2003, available at www.icrc.org (accessed 6 November 2006). See also the account of ICRC visits in Nelson Mandela, *Long Walk*

to Freedom (Boston: Little, Brown, 1994), pp. 357–359, 361, 427.

5. Philippe Gaillard, "Rwanda 1994: 'La vraie vie est absente,'" talk given at the International Museum of the Red Cross and Red Crescent, Geneva, 18 October 1994. Available at www.icrc.org (accessed 8 September 2005).

6. Human Rights Watch, "Turkey: Condemn Threats on Human Rights Defenders," available at hrw.org (accessed 28 November 2006).

7. Elaine Scarry, *The Body in Pain: The Making and Unmaking of the World* (New York: Oxford University Press, 1985), pp. 27–59.

8. See Human Rights Watch, "Essential Background: Overview of Human Rights Issues in Turkey," available at hrw.org (accessed 26 November 2006).

3. BURNOUT

1. Mani Sheik, Maria Isabel Gutierrez, Paul Bolton, Paul Spiegel, Michael Thieren, and Gilbert Burnham, "Deaths among Humanitarian Workers," *BMJ: British Medical Journal* 321 (2000): 166.

2. Press release, interview with Anne Brüschweiler, September 1, 2004. Available at "Press releases 21/09/2004," www.micr.ch (accessed 8 September 2005).

3. Volunteers among young people today, it has been argued, illustrate a structural change in volunteering as a whole. As Walter Rehberg writes in a study of the motivations of international volunteers: "'Old' volunteering is closely connected to certain social milieus such as religious or political communities, involves a long-term and often membership-based commitment, and for which altruistic motivations play a key role for the involvement of individuals. 'New' volunteering, on the other hand, is more project oriented, and volunteers have specific expectations as to form, time, and content of their involvement. . . . Young volunteers are not particularly loyal to organizations, tend to be rather choosy about what they do, and expect some personal benefit from their volunteering." See Walter Rehberg, "Altruistic Individualists: Motivations for International Volunteering among Young Adults in Switzerland," *Voluntas: International Journal of Voluntary and Nonprofit Organizations* 16, no. 2 (June 2005): 109–122.

4. Plato, *The Republic,* IV.439E, trans. B. Jowett (Oxford: Clarendon, 1888), p. 132.

5. Museum of the International Red Cross, Press release, available at "Press releases 21/09/2004," www.micr.ch (accessed 8 September 2005).

6. Alan Cumyn, *Burridge Unbound* (Toronto: McClelland and Stewart, 2000), p. 138.

7. Kenneth Cain, Heidi Postlewait, and Andrew Thomson, *Emergency Sex and Other Desperate Measures: A True Story from Hell on Earth* (New York: Miramax, 2004), p. 88.

8. Kenneth Cain, Interview with Robin Lustig, *The Connection*, WBUR Boston and National Public Radio, 9 August 2004.

9. Helen Fielding, *Cause Celeb* (New York: Penguin, 1994), p. 3.

10. Ibid., p. 250.

11. Mark Jacobs, "The Egg Queen Rises," in *Living on the Edge: Fiction by Peace Corps Writers,* ed. John Coyne (Willimantic, Conn.: Curbstone, 1999), p. 187.

12. Deborah Scroggins, *Emma's War: An Aid Worker, a Warlord, Radical Islam, and the Politics of Oil—A True Story of Love and Death in Sudan* (New York: Pantheon, 2002), p. 65.

13. Cain, Postlewait, and Thomson, *Emergency Sex and Other Desperate Measures,* p. 37.

14. David Rieff, *A Bed for the Night: Humanitarianism in Crisis* (New York: Simon and Schuster, 2002), p. 274.

15. Fielding, *Cause Celeb,* p. 145.

16. Anthony Loyd, *My War Gone By, I Miss It So* (New York: Atlantic Monthly Press, 1999), p. 54.

17. Cain, Postlewait, and Thomson, *Emergency Sex and Other Desperate Measures*, p. 9.

18. Elie Wiesel, "A Tribute to Human Rights," in *The Universal Declaration of Human Rights: Fifty Years and Beyond*, ed. Y. Danieli et al. (Amityville, N.Y.: Baywood, 1999), p. 3. Upendra Baxi, *The Future of Human Rights* (Oxford: Oxford University Press, 2002), pp. 1–2. Michael Ignatieff, *Human Rights as Politics and Idolatry*, ed. Amy Gutmann (Princeton: Princeton University Press, 2001), pp. 5, 53.

19. Johannes Morsink, *The Universal Declaration of Human Rights: Origins, Drafting, and Intent* (Philadelphia: University of Pennsylvania Press, 1999), p. 20.

20. Margaret Keck and Kathryn Sikkink, *Activists beyond Borders* (Ithaca: Cornell University Press, 1998), p. 10.

21. For more work questioning the current frames and institutions of human rights and humanitarianism, see Terry, *The Paradox of Humanitarian Action;* Maren, *The Road to Hell;* and *And Justice for All? The Claims of Human Rights*, a special issue of *SAQ: South Atlantic Quarterly* (July 2004).

22. Baxi, *The Future of Human Rights*, pp. 63, 122, 132, 122, italics in the original. For instance, "the struggle against homelessness and for shelter, in the 1998 United Nations Social Summit at Istanbul, becomes a series of mandates for the construction industries

and urban developers," and sustainable development "becomes an instrument of policy for the promotion and protection of corporate governance practices of 'greenwashing'" (141).

Criticisms like Baxi's are sometimes characterized as part of the conflict between the three "generations" of human rights. The first generation of human rights ("first" in the chronological sense), born of the Enlightenment, emphasizes civil liberties, focusing primarily upon political participation and the protection of individuals from excessive state power. The second generation, emerging with socialism and the rise of organized labor, encompasses social and economic equality. Concentrating on the rights individuals have to all those things necessary to the full realization of personhood, including health and employment, second-generation rights emphasize not what the state should refrain from doing *to* its citizens but rather what it must do *for* them. The third generation of human rights includes group or collective rights, such as the right to self-determination, which were so crucial to the mid-twentieth-century solidarity movements that threw off the shackles of colonial oppression in Africa and Asia.

While many believe these generations are as complementary as the principles of "liberty, equality, and fraternity," there are also those who experience their relationship as a contradiction. Some liberals argue, for instance, that only rights of the first generation are true rights. They argue that second-generation rights, such as the rights to adequate housing, education, and protection against unemployment, are for many nations unrealizable even if one assumes the goodwill of the state—unlike, say, the litigable right not to be detained indefinitely without charges. Confusing *preferences* about the distribution of social goods with *rights* due to individuals, they contend, leads among other things to a proliferation of unenforceable rights and to irreconcilable conflict between entitlement claims that, by the very nature of rights rhetoric, all trump one another. In other words, as Amartya Sen characterizes the position, for something to be a right rather than simply a desirable goal, it must be both feasible (accomplishable for all) and justiciable (enforceable in a court of law). See Amartya Sen, "Human Rights and Development," in *Development as a Human Right: Legal, Political, and Economic Dimensions,* ed. Bård Andreassen and Stephen P. Marks (Cambridge, Mass.: Harvard University Press, 2006), pp. 1–8.

Critics of such liberal arguments (like Sen) respond in two primary ways. First, they maintain that the liberal characterization of first- and second-generation rights is simply incorrect. As an empirical matter, Sen notes, first-generation rights have struggled with the same problems of feasibility that second-generation rights have. And it's just not true, Stephen Marks and Bård Andreassen add, that second-generation rights "must be provided by the state, that they are costly and lead to an overgrown state apparatus, and that they must be fully justiciable to have the status of rights." See their Introduction in *Development as a Human Right,* pp. xiv–xvii. Second, critics accuse liberals of promoting a minimalist conception of negative rights and civil liberties that allows for human rights only when they do not contradict free-market capitalism and the principles of neoliberal globalization—principles that have, according to many, effectively disenfranchised populations throughout the world. See note 23 below for more.

23. See Curt Goering, "Amnesty International and Economic, Social, and Cultural Rights," in *Ethics in Action: The Ethical Challenges of International Human Rights Nongovernmental Organizations,* ed. Daniel Bell

and Jean-Marc Coicaud (Cambridge: Cambridge University Press, 2007), pp. 204–217. Relatedly, see Andreassen and Marks, *Development as a Human Right: Legal, Political, and Economic Dimensions*.

In recent years Human Rights Watch has also made it a priority to defend economic, social, and cultural rights. It focuses on situations when "arbitrary or discriminatory governmental conduct lies behind an economic, social and cultural rights violation." HRW has defended, for instance, the basic labor rights of workers in Mexico's maquiladoras but has done so in strategic, targeted ways: in one report, by condemning the discriminatory practice of requiring female workers to undergo pregnancy testing. See HRW, "Economic, Social, and Cultural Rights" at www.hrw.org (accessed 2 February 2007). Critics argue that this approach is too narrow and that influential organizations like HRW should speak more generally to the problem of inequitable distribution of resources. HRW defends its practice by arguing that their methodology of investigating and reporting ("naming and shaming") would be ineffective in such contexts. For a spirited debate on this topic, see the exchange between Kenneth Roth, executive director of HRW, and Neera Chandhoke in *Ethics*

in Action, pp. 169–203. The debate between the two
brings to my mind this famous line from Anatole
France's *The Red Lily:* the poor "must labour in the
face of the majestic equality of the laws, which for-
bid rich and poor alike to sleep under the bridges, to
beg in the streets, and to steal their bread" (Anatole
France, *The Red Lily,* trans. Winifred Stephens [New
York: Dodd, Mead, 1924], p. 91). See note 22 above
for more.

24. David Kennedy, *The Dark Sides of Virtue: Reassessing
International Humanitarianism* (Princeton: Princeton
University Press, 2004), p. 8. Upendra Baxi writes:
"When human rights languages steadily supplant all
other ethical languages, when almost each and every
'new' social movement tends to coalesce with the
logics and paralogics of human rights, when all resistance to formations of power begins to present itself
as morally *worthy* only when it shapes itself in human rights talk, the politics *of* human rights brings to
us both human hope and hazards. The hope lies in
the construction of visions of an 'ethical' state. The
hazards lie in the acts of mystification of the modes
of production of human misery and suffering" (Baxi,
The Future of Human Rights, p. ix).

25. Kennedy, *The Dark Sides of Virtue,* p. 9. Much of Ken-

nedy's skepticism, he explains, comes from his position as a lawyer. As he told me, "Lawyers looking at any other piece of legislation or any other legal regime, whether it's drug labeling regulation or criminal law or whatever, have a fair amount of skepticism about the way legal pronouncements transform themselves immediately into social effects, about the paradoxical and sometimes perverse effects that can happen when you try to regulate in a new area, and just the difficulties of translating aspirations into effects through law." It can be salutary for the movement, he believes, to bring this skepticism to human rights.

26. Makau Mutua, *Human Rights: A Political and Cultural Critique* (Philadelphia: University of Pennsylvania Press, 2002), pp. 2, 73. Against claims like Mutua's, Johannes Morsink argues that Article 29 of the Universal Declaration ("Everyone has duties to the community in which alone the free and full development of his personality is possible") represents the strong "communitarian" views of the many delegates from around the world who drafted this foundational document (Morsink, *Universal Declaration of Human Rights*, p. 335).

27. For more on the special difficulties of human rights law and discourse in Africa, see Abdullahi A. An-

Na'im, "The Legal Protection of Human Rights in Africa: How To Do More with Less," in *Human Rights: Concepts, Contests, Contingencies,* ed. Austin Sarat and Thomas Kearns (Ann Arbor: University of Michigan Press, 2001), pp. 89–116.

28. Rieff, *A Bed for the Night,* p. 274. See also James Orbinski's 1999 Nobel Lecture on behalf of Médecins Sans Frontières, available at nobelprize.org/peace/laureates/1999/msf-lecture.html (accessed 22 December 2006). For Rieff, the distinction between human rights work and humanitarianism properly conceived is crucial: "What I like about humanitarian action is what humanitarians themselves like least about it, which is its limitations, its modesty. . . . It is this wonderful phrase of an International Committee of the Red Cross official: 'Humanitarian action is trying to bring a measure of humanity, always insufficient, into situations that shouldn't exist.'" In contrast, "the notion of human rights is a waste of hope and the phrase 'international community' is wishful thinking. . . . There has been no revolution of moral concern. There are just a lot of people who want consoling mythologies about how things are really going to work out." David Rieff, quoted in Denise Leith, *Bear-*

ing Witness: The Lives of War Correspondents and Photo-journalists (Sydney: Random House Australia, 2004), pp. 294–295.

29. Nuruddin Farah, *Links* (New York: Penguin, 2004), p. 124.

30. Relatedly, see Lyal S. Sunga, "Dilemmas Facing NGOs in Coalition-Occupied Iraq," in Bell and Coicaud, *Ethics in Action,* pp. 99–116.

31. Nuruddin Farah, *Gifts* (New York: Penguin, 1999), pp. 22, 196, 23, 194, 196.

32. Ken Saro-Wiwa, "Night Ride," in his collection *A Forest of Flowers* (Essex: Longman Group, 1995), p. 116. On the range of challenges to the integrity of development NGOs, Peter Willetts writes: "The dangers include projects being tailored to the concerns of the donors, new NGOs being established solely to attract funds, and NGO leaders being co-opted onto official bodies. At the extreme, in a few countries an NGO may be established by the government to infiltrate and gather information on the NGO community." See Willetts, "Introduction," in *The Conscience of the World: The Influence of Non-Governmental Organisations in the UN System,* ed. Peter Willetts (Washington, D.C.: Brookings Institution, 1996), p. 6.

33. Jonathan Shay, *Achilles in Vietnam: Combat Trauma and the Undoing of Character* (New York: Simon and Schuster, 1994), p. 20.

34. Heidi Postlewait, Interview with Robin Lustig, *The Connection*, WBUR Boston and National Public Radio, 9 August 2004.

35. Brayne here was referring to a quotation from a survivor of the siege of Sarajevo recorded in a BBC documentary produced by Alan Little and Peter Burdin, "My Beloved Sarajevo," first broadcast in October 2005 and now available at news.bbc.co.uk/ 2/hi/programmes/documentary_archive (accessed 11 June 2006).

36. For a relevant analysis of the UN bureaucracy, see Michael Barnett, "The UN Security Council, Indifference, and Genocide in Rwanda," *Cultural Anthropology* 12, no. 4 (November 1997): 551–578. For more on dysfunction in organizations that manage violence, see James Dawes, *The Language of War* (Cambridge, Mass.: Harvard University Press, 2002), pp. 167–191. Barnett was one of the political officers assigned to Rwanda at the US mission to the United Nations during the genocide in 1994. The UN failed to intervene then, he argues, because it "had more to lose by taking action and being associated with another failure

than it did by not taking action and allowing the genocide in Rwanda" (561). In other words, the priority the bureaucracy places on protecting itself from risk, so that it can survive and continue to promote its vision of the good, means that it must often fail to promote its vision of the good. Bureaucracies are inherently conservative in this sense. When we spoke, however, Barnett emphasized his belief that the UN was especially risk-averse, from the top of the organization to the bottom. The phrase that's always used there, he said, is that you only push for "what the traffic will bear." In other words, "you just don't propose things that you think will get rejected. You just don't. There's absolutely no incentive for proposing anything that might be viewed as mildly heretical or controversial, because if you do the consequences can be severe. You lose credibility, you lose face."

37. David Loquercio, Mark Hammersley, and Ben Emmens, "Understanding and Addressing Staff Turnover in Humanitarian Agencies," paper 55, June 2006 (London: Humanitarian Practice Network), p. 9. David Forsythe writes that at the ICRC, "on average, for each 100 new staff recruited, 75 percent had left at the end of three years." See David P. Forsythe, *The Hu-*

manitarians: The International Committee of the Red Cross (Cambridge: Cambridge University Press, 2005).

38. Mary Anderson, "'You Save My Life Today, But for What Tomorrow?': Some Moral Dilemmas of Humanitarian Aid," in *Hard Choices: Moral Dilemmas in Humanitarian Intervention,* ed. Jonathan Moore (Oxford: Rowman and Littlefield, 1998), pp. 151, 149.

39. Mark Walkup, "Policy Dysfunction in Humanitarian Organizations: The Role of Coping Strategies, Institutions, and Organizational Culture," *Journal of Refugee Studies* 10, no. 1 (1997): 44, 46.

40. Matthew Bolton, "Becoming an Aid Worker: an Experienced Professional Explains How It's Done," *Transitions Abroad Magazine,* September–October 2004. Available at www.transitionsabroad.com (accessed 8 September 2005).

41. A note on misfits and adventurers: in one preliminary study of people who intervened during the Holocaust, a researcher concluded that "a spirit of adventurousness" and "a sense of being socially marginal" were key personality traits related to altruistic behavior. See Perry London, "The Rescuers: Motivational Hypotheses about Christians Who Saved Jews from the Nazis," in *Altruism and Helping Behavior: Social Psychological Studies of Some Antecedents and Conse-*

quences, ed. J. Macaulay and L. Berkowitz (New York: Academic Press, 1970), pp. 241–250.

42. Shashi Tharoor, quoted in Ben McGrath, "The Diplomats: Just Whistle," *New Yorker,* 20 and 27 December 2004.

43. Charles Perrow, *Normal Accidents* (Princeton: Princeton University Press, 1999).

4. STORYTELLING

1. John Coyne, Preface, in Coyne, ed., *Living on the Edge: Fiction by Peace Corps Writers* (Willimantic, Conn.: Curbstone Press, 1999), p. x.

2. Fred Ritchin, introduction, *Magnum Photos* (Paris: Editions Nathan, 1997), p. 1; English translation available at the Magnum Photos Web Site, "History of Magnum," www.magnumphotos.com (accessed 18 May 2006).

3. Harold Evans, *War Stories: Reporting in the Time of Conflict, from the Crimea to Iraq* (Boston: Bunker Hill, 2003), p. 55.

4. Harold Evans, *Pictures on a Page* (New York: Holt, Rinehart and Winston, 1978), p. 286.

5. John G. Morris, *Get the Picture: A Personal History of Photojournalism* (Chicago: University of Chicago Press, 2002), p. 293.

6. Writing of war photography during Vietnam, John Berger argues more bleakly: moments of agony "are discontinuous with all other moments. They exist by themselves. But the reader who has been arrested by the photograph may tend to feel this discontinuity as his own personal moral inadequacy. *And as soon as this happens, even his sense of shock is dispersed:* his own moral inadequacy may now shock him as much as the crimes being committed in the war. Either he shrugs off this sense of inadequacy as being only too familiar, or else he thinks of performing a kind of penance—of which the purest example would be to make a contribution to Oxfam or to UNICEF. In both cases, the issue of the war which has caused that moment is effectively depoliticised. The picture becomes evidence of the general human condition. It accuses nobody and everybody." See the essay "Photographs of Agony," in Berger, *About Looking* (New York: Vintage International, 1991; orig. pub. 1980), pp. 43–44.

7. Susan Sontag, *Regarding the Pain of Others* (New York: Farrar, Straus and Giroux, 2003), p. 112.

8. Peter Maass, *Love Thy Neighbor* (New York: Alfred A. Knopf, 1996), p. 54.

9. *Truth and Reconciliation Commission of South Africa Report,* vol. 1 (London: Macmillan, 1998), pp. 144, 112.

10. Ibid., vol. 5, p. 444.

11. Ibid., vol. 5, p. 356.

12. Eric Stover, *The Witnesses: War Crimes and the Promise of Justice in The Hague* (Philadelphia: University of Pennsylvania Press, 2005), p. 88. Elsewhere Stover cautions against "the compelling fantasy of a fast, cathartic cure," citing contemporary psychotherapeutic examination of the dangers associated with "injudicious catharsis." See *My Neighbor, My Enemy: Justice and Community in the Aftermath of Mass Atrocity,* ed. Eric Stover and Harvey Weinstein (Cambridge: Cambridge University Press, 2004), p. 13.

13. Gillian Slovo, *Red Dust* (New York: Norton, 2000), p. 65.

14. Antjie Krog, *Country of My Skull* (New York: Three Rivers, 1998), pp. 95, 93, 94.

15. Slovo, *Red Dust,* p. 227.

16. Kay Schaffer and Sidonie Smith, *Human Rights and Narrated Lives: The Ethics of Recognition* (New York: Palgrave Macmillan, 2004), p. 78. See also Fiona Ross, "Bearing Witness to Ripples of Pain," in *World Memory: Personal Trajectories in Global Time,* ed. Jill Bennett and Rosanne Kennedy (New York: Palgrave Macmillan, 2003), pp. 143–159. On truth, representation, and healing—with special, more generous reference to Krog—see Mark Sanders, "Truth, Telling,

Questioning: The Truth and Reconciliation Commission, Antjie Krog's *Country of My Skull,* and Literature after Apartheid," *Modern Fiction Studies* 46, no. 1 (Spring 2000): 13–41.

17. Krog, *Country of My Skull,* p. 312.

18. Thandi Shezi, quoted in Pamela Sethunya Dube, "The Story of Thandi Shezi," in *Commissioning the Past: Understanding South Africa's Truth and Reconciliation Commission,* ed. Deborah Posel and Graeme Simpson (Johannesburg: Witwatersrand University Press, 2002), p. 128.

19. Ping Chong, *Children of War,* final draft dated 6 December 2002, provided by author and director Ping Chong, copyright © Ping Chong and Co., 2002.

20. See, for instance, Douglas McGray, "Out of the Mouths of Babes," *Washington Post Magazine,* 2 February 2003, pp. 10–30.

21. Haviv's comment about soldiers "acting up" raises important questions. As Thomas Keenan asks elsewhere, what good is "naming and shaming" when perpetrators see being caught on film not as a form of exposure but rather as a photo-op? If "mobilizing shame" is a primary strategy in human rights work, what are we to do when perpetrators are shameless? See Thomas Keenan, "Mobilizing Shame," *SAQ: South*

Atlantic Quarterly 103, nos. 2–3 (Spring–Summer 2004): 435–449.

22. Maass, *Love Thy Neighbor,* pp. 49, 48.

23. Jeri Laber, *The Courage of Strangers* (New York: Public Affairs, 2002), pp. 195–196.

24. The bulk of academic research on representation and human rights tends to focus on nonfiction accounts (memoirs, reportage, legal and political documents, and so on). See Schaffer and Smith's important *Human Rights and Narrated Lives.* There are, however, notable exceptions focusing on fictional accounts. See portions of *Human Rights and Narrated Lives;* Barbara Harlow's *Barred: Women, Writing, and Political Detention* (Hanover: Wesleyan University Press, 1992); and Joseph Slaughter and Jennifer Wenzel, "Letters of the Law: Women, Human Rights, and Epistolary Literature," in *Women, Gender, and Human Rights: A Global Perspective,* ed. Marjorie Agosín (New Brunswick, N.J.: Rutgers University Press, 2001), pp. 289–311. See also Joseph Slaughter, "Enabling Fictions and Novel Subjects: The *Bildungsroman* and International Human Rights Law," *PMLA* 125, no. 5 (October 2006): 1405–23.

25. Krog, *Country of My Skull,* p. 24.

26. Slovo, *Red Dust,* pp. 336–337.

27. Kathy Reichs, *Grave Secrets* (New York: Scribner, 2002), pp. 300, 313.

28. Slovo told me, in fact, that she turned away from her successful career as a mystery writer in favor of novels like *Red Dust* precisely because of the way the genre's requirement of narrative completion ("the pure form of the mystery novel," as she put it, "whereby justice is done, signed, sealed, and delivered") interfered with exploring complex truths.

29. The belief that justice functions as a narrative form which falsifies traumatic experience has its foundations (as does the human rights novel itself) in the more general contradictions of existential literature, which attempts to express the nausea inspired by life's "utter shapelessness" through the shaping form of the novel. See Frank Kermode, *The Sense of an Ending: Studies in the Theory of Fiction* (Oxford: Oxford University Press, 1966), p. 145.

30. John Treat, *Writing Ground Zero: Japanese Literature and the Atomic Bomb* (Chicago: University of Chicago Press, 1995), pp. 43, 39; see also pp. 40–41, 81.

31. Claude Lanzmann, "The Obscenity of Understanding," in *Trauma: Explorations in Memory,* ed. Cathy Caruth (Baltimore: Johns Hopkins University Press, 1995), p. 204.

32. On the part standing for the whole in war representation, see Elaine Scarry, *The Body in Pain: The Making and Unmaking of the World* (New York: Oxford University Press, 1985), pp. 60–161.

33. Michael Ondaatje, *Anil's Ghost* (New York: Vintage, 2000), p. 275.

34. See Fredric Jameson on allegory in "third-world texts": Jameson, "Third-World Literature in the Era of Multinational Capitalism," *Social Text* 15 (Fall 1986): 69. On allegory in Coetzee specifically, with particular attention to critiques of his political authenticity and commitment to place, see Ian Glenn, "Nadine Gordimer, J. M. Coetzee, and the Politics of Interpretation," *SAQ: South Atlantic Quarterly* 93, no. 1 (Winter 1994): 11–32. Nadine Gordimer describes his authorial urge to allegory as "stately fastidiousness": Gordimer, "The Idea of Gardening," *New York Review of Books,* 2 February 1984, p. 3. Defending Coetzee against the common charge that his abstracted dehistoricization is quietistic in the face of real suffering, Samuel Durrant argues that Coetzee's texts use the allegorical mode to respect pain by refusing "to translate that suffering into a narrative": Durrant, "Bearing Witness to Apartheid: J. M. Coetzee's Inconsolable Works of Mourning," *Contemporary Literature* 40, no. 3 (Fall 1999): 431.

35. Douglas Unger, *Voices from Silence* (New York: St. Martin's, 1995), p. 283.

36. Lawrence Thornton, *Tales from the Blue Archives* (New York: Doubleday, 1997), p. 4.

37. Ibid., p. 155.

38. Ibid., pp. 155–156, 263.

39. Ernest J. Gaines, *A Lesson before Dying* (New York: Vintage, 1993), pp. 8, 256.

40. Dave Eggers, *What Is the What: The Autobiography of Valentino Achak Deng* (San Francisco: McSweeney's, 2006).

41. The final quotation is from an interview conducted by Lena Sallin and used in a case study in the Local Capacities for Peace Project, sponsored by the Collaborative for Development Action (1995).

42. Joan Richter, "The Ones Left Behind," in Coyne, ed., *Living on the Edge*, p. 210.

43. Emmanuel Dongala, author of *Johnny Mad Dog*, a novel about a child soldier in the Congolese civil war, emphasized this point in our discussion of the good and ill of humanitarian interventions:

"For a stricken individual in a disaster area, the arrival of a humanitarian NGO is like a gift fallen from heaven. During the Congolese civil war, I witnessed the joy which illuminated the faces of women when one of these humanitarian NGOs arrived in the spontaneous campsite where we took refuge. After agonizing for days because their children had nothing to eat or because they were suffering from malaria or severe diarrhea, these women had a deep sense of gratitude towards these humanitarian workers, without whom their children might have certainly died. I was happy they were there; they probably saved my life too. . . .

"[But] when I started looking closely at the way many of these humanitarian organizations operate, I came to the conclusion that whatever positive work they may do, it is offset by the negative aspect of their practice. . . . What I find most egregious is the way they act during emergencies, when their appeal for donors' generosity is accompanied by graphic images of misery which strip the people suffering of their dignity, images which are not far from voyeurism. . . . When the name Africa comes up, immediately poverty, diseases, drought and other natural disasters jump to the mind of the Western interlocutor, totally unaware that Africa is also a continent where people live, marry, make love, have children, laugh, dance and live normal lives."

44. Ondaatje, *Anil's Ghost,* p. 44.

45. Anne-christine d'Adesky, *Under the Bone* (New York: Farrar, Straus and Giroux, 1994), pp. 251–252.

46. J. M. Coetzee, *Waiting for the Barbarians* (New York: Penguin, 1999), p. 63.

47. Ibid., p. 132.

48. Ibid., p. 133.

49. On the magistrate's intimacy with the barbarian girl, see, for instance, Barbara Eckstein, "The Body, the Word, and the State: J. M. Coetzee's *Waiting for the Barbarians*," *Novel: A Forum on Fiction* 22, no. 2 (Winter 1989): 188–189. See also Ali Behdad, "Eroticism, Colonialism, and Violence," in *Violence, Identity, and Self-determination*, ed. Hent de Vries and Samuel Weber (Stanford: Stanford University Press, 1997), pp. 201–207.

50. Unger, *Voices from Silence*, pp. 140, 149.

51. D'Adesky, *Under the Bone*, p. 144.

52. Alan Cumyn, *Man of Bone* (Toronto: McClelland and Stewart, 2002), p. 186.

53. Michael Ignatieff, *Charlie Johnson in the Flames* (New York: Grove, 2003), p. 50. Relatedly, see "Dealing with the Trauma of Covering War: Excerpts from a Conference," *Nieman Reports* 53, no. 2 (Summer 1999): 24–27.

54. Farnoosh Moshiri, *The Bathhouse* (Boston: Beacon, 2003), pp. 87–88.

55. Ibid., p. 103.

56. Ondaatje, *Anil's Ghost,* pp. 113, 22.

57. Coetzee, *Waiting for the Barbarians,* e.g., pp. 4, 93, 95.

58. Ibid., p. 70. On language in *Waiting for the Barbarians,* see Michael Valdez Moses, "The Mark of Empire: Writing, History, and Torture in Coetzee's *Waiting for the Barbarians,*" *Kenyon Review* 15, no. 1 (Winter 1993): 115–127. See also Susan Van Zanten Gallagher, "Torture and the Novel: J. M. Coetzee's *Waiting for the Barbarians,*" *Contemporary Literature* 29, no. 2 (Summer 1988): 277–285; and Benita Parry, "Speech and Silence in the Fictions of J. M. Coetzee," in *Critical Perspectives on J. M. Coetzee,* ed. Graham Huggan and Stephen Watson (New York: St. Martin's, 1996), pp. 37–65.

59. Marta Traba, *Mothers and Shadows,* trans. Jo Labanyi (London: Readers International, 1986), p. 80. On linguistic failure in Marta Traba, see Emily Tomlinson, "Rewriting Fictions of Power: The Texts of Luisa Valenzuela and Marta Traba," *Modern Language Review* 93, no. 3 (July 1998): 695–709.

60. Edwidge Danticat, *The Dew Breaker* (New York: Alfred A. Knopf, 2004), p. 61.

61. Tahar Djaout, *The Last Summer of Reason* (St. Paul, Minn.: Ruminator, 2001).

62. Isabel Allende, *Of Love and Shadows,* trans. Margaret Sayers Peden (New York: Alfred A. Knopf, 1987), p. 230.

63. Nuruddin Farah, *Sweet and Sour Milk* (St. Paul, Minn.: Graywolf, 1992), p. 137.

64. Lawrence Thornton, *Imagining Argentina* (New York: Doubleday, 1987), p. 78.

65. Omar Rivabella, *Requiem for a Woman's Soul* (New York: Random House, 1986), p. 116.

66. Ignatieff, *Charlie Johnson in the Flames,* pp. 94, 179.

67. Victoria Brittain and Gillian Slovo, *Guantánamo: Honor Bound to Defend Freedom* (New York version), manuscript provided by the author, copyright © 2007 Gillian Slovo, pp. 21, 22, 30.

68. Hong Ying, *Summer of Betrayal,* trans. Martha Avery (New York: Grove, 1997), p. 127.

69. Maurice Blanchot, *The Writing of the Disaster,* trans. Ann Smock (Lincoln: University of Nebraska Press, 1995).

70. Marguerite Feitlowitz, *A Lexicon of Terror: Argentina and the Legacies of Torture* (Oxford: Oxford University Press, 1998), p. 61.

71. Scarry, *The Body in Pain,* pp. 3–26.

72. Quoted in Feitlowitz, *A Lexicon of Terror,* p. 20.

73. Ann Patchett, *Bel Canto* (New York: Perennial, 2001), p. 311.

74. Scarry, *The Body in Pain,* p. 50.

75. Rivabella, *Requiem for a Woman's Soul,* p. 63.

AFTERWORD

1. Donatella Lorch, "In Rwanda, a Time to Weep and a Time to Wed," *New York Times,* 23 January 1995, p. A4.

ACKNOWLEDGMENTS

I would like to express my gratitude to and admiration for all those who appear in this book. I would also like to thank the generous institutions that supported this project, including the American Council of Learned Societies, Harvard University's Society of Fellows and the Milton Fund, and Macalester College.

An early version of Chapter 2 appeared as "Atrocity and Interrogation," *Critical Inquiry* 30 (Winter 2004): 249–266. I am grateful to the editors for permission to republish.